PRUE LEITH

prue

PRUE LEITH

Prue

MY ALL-TIME FAVOURITE RECIPES

bluebird
books for life

Introduction

When I gave up writing cookbooks to concentrate on novels, I found, somewhat to my surprise, that food kept creeping into my fiction. Characters would turn out to be chefs or cooks or restaurateurs, and somehow a great deal of cooking went on.

But I still had no thoughts of returning to cookery writing, and it is now over twenty years since I wrote, or even co-authored, a cookbook. It wasn't just that I hadn't the time to write both cookbooks and novels, it was also that I felt stale. I knew I could knock out another reliable, solid cookbook, but I didn't feel inspired. Somehow, with all the years of cookery writing, catering, teaching and restaurants, I'd lost that deep interest that makes a great cookery writer. And anyway, there were wonderful younger cookery writers appearing, with new ideas, new interests, new ingredients, new and imaginative takes on the art, necessity and science that is cooking.

I was content with leaving the field to others doing a brilliant job. My time had come and gone, and that was that, I thought.

Until I joined *The Great British Bake Off*. I couldn't, I discovered, spend three months in a tent full of totally committed bakers and NOT want to get back into food writing. It started with me asking for the occasional recipe and swiftly led on to my doing far more baking in those three months than I'd done in the last twenty years. It wasn't just the bakers that set me off experimenting, testing, writing. Paul Hollywood has made baking his own, and his image absolutely reflects his personality: a lovely man who likes cars, bikes and football – and fairy cakes. Sandi Toksvig is a keen baker too. Only Noel Fielding doesn't bake. But I bet he will.

I began to feel that long-forgotten excitement of inventing recipes and returning to old favourites. It has been pure joy to be back in the kitchen, sometimes adding new twists to recipes I've always loved. I brought in the brilliant young cook Georgina Fuggle to help me whittle down the selection and test. Since then, most of the struggles have been to keep it down to a hundred or so recipes.

The Colourful Cook

I have to admit this book doesn't have a theme. It's not all about health, or cakes, or a national cuisine, or speedy cooking, or economy, or posh showing off. It's not 'all about' anything. At one point, I thought it might be all about leftovers because my (newish – we married in 2016) husband, John, when asked if he eats like a king because he's married a *Bake Off* queen, says, 'No, it's mostly leftovers. I've hardly eaten the same thing twice in all the time we have been together. She just opens the fridge, and fifteen minutes later we have something amazing for supper.'

He exaggerates of course. There'd be no leftovers if I hadn't done some primary cooking the day before. And it's not always amazing. But it is true that I love leftovers. Most good cooks do. It allows one to be creative, save money and make something delicious, all at the same time. My husband's favourite 'telly supper' is a plate of handheld bits made from leftovers, suitably disguised. We call it Clockwork Plate (see page 72) because you start at the top and eat your way right round.

There are other dishes inspired by leftovers. But really the recipes are for the most delicious things I've encountered in over fifty years of working in the food world and the best recipes I've cooked at home for family and friends. There are recipes from my childhood in South Africa, dishes my catering company excelled at, signature dishes from my restaurant, the food my children loved thirty years ago, and ideas I've blatantly stolen from other cooks (with permission and a credit, I promise!).

A Lifetime of Good Food

I've always been greedy, and am probably more so now, with a thickening waistline and little chance of ever seeing eleven stone again. But the way we eat, and what we eat, has changed hugely in my lifetime. Certainly the classic French cream-and-butter-laden dishes of my youth now appear less often on my table, though a few of the best of them are in this book. When I opened my restaurant, in 1969, it was the first posh restaurant here with its menus written in English. To the French-dominated restaurant world, the fact that neither customers nor kitchen staff had a clue what *faisan à la souveroff* or *noisettes d'agneau* meant was neither here nor there. I'm old enough, I'm sorry to say, to remember when chefs would say, 'If it's not in Escoffier's *Guide culinaire*, it is not cuisine.' But the rigidity of classic *haute cuisine* gradually gave way to the excitement of the seventies *nouvelle cuisine* revolution, when top French chefs at last threw off the shackles of the great Escoffier and dared to invent; to use newly available ingredients; to produce well designed, colourful, balanced, individual plates, instead of sauce-covered brown food in serving dishes. Of course this fashion was often abused, with customers complaining of 'a little bit of nothing on a big white plate: a restaurateur's dream of portion control' but the good ones gave diners an astonishing experience: an explosion of flavours, contrasting textures and surprising combinations, arrived at by a constant search for absolute perfection.

The inspiration for some of my recipes does come from those great chefs, albeit simplified. All good cooks like to show off occasionally – having a tableful of dinner guests saying 'Wow!' is a very good feeling.

Food is a matter of fashion, as well as feeding, so eventually *nouvelle cuisine* gave way to a blast of Asian flavours and 'fusion food', where combining East and West became acceptable; then to Middle Eastern dishes, Spanish tapas, and now street food from every continent, generally cooked by genuine enthusiasts. The internet has made a difference too, with entrepreneurs delivering recipe boxes of ingredients ready to be assembled or cooked in minutes. And top restaurants are no longer too grand to have their gastronomy delivered to our doors by scooter.

But simple family food is what I mostly cook today. In the eighties there was a great fashion for 'comfort food', and suddenly bangers and mash, fish cakes, pasta al pesto, and a lot more besides, became fashionable in gastropubs and restaurants – and of course at home, where comfort begins and ends.

I'm excited by lots of modern food, especially the trend for sharing dishes or ordering a selection of small cicchetti (Venetian-style small plates) to pick and choose from. Plonking platters of shareable food in the middle of a table and watching the contents disappear is very satisfying.

Needless to say, very little fancy restaurant food would be dished up by me at home in my catering days. I was running my business, which consisted of Leith's School of Food and Wine; Leith's Restaurant; and the catering company (party and event catering and contract catering for venues like Glyndebourne, the Orient Express train and the Edinburgh International Conference Centre). I would be in our London flat during the week, while Rayne, my writer husband, stayed in our house in the Cotswolds, joining me for one night to eat at Leith's restaurant. On Fridays I'd scamper back in order to be home before the children returned from weekly boarding school.

So, if you asked my children, now in their forties, what they ate as children, I think they'd remember the Sunday roast, sausages and mash, spag bol, shepherd's pie and veg out of the garden. I used to make my own sausages, fish fingers, yoghurt, ice cream, pâtés and jams. It would not have occurred to me to buy these things. I do remember my son Daniel, at about seven, once saying 'Mum, it's my birthday. Can't I have sausages like we have at school? And white sliced bread?'

A Modern Way to Eat

If I had my way, we'd all eat less meat, but of much better quality. Nothing factory-farmed, and from free-range, grass-fed animals, etc. And we'd consume the whole beast, nose to tail. I'm of the generation that really likes to eat kidneys, liver, bone marrow. But I'm aware that most young cooks, unless they are chefs, shudder at the thought. So I have restricted myself to three recipes, which I dearly hope you will try.

We'd also eat heaps more veg. Indeed, I was tempted to make this book a mission about sustainable, healthy food. But since this is a tour of my life in food, I could hardly leave out all the creamy, booze-laden, absolutely delicious dishes from the past that I still love. On occasion, anything is forgivable.

Because I eat absolutely everything, I used to be very bad at remembering who is veggie, gluten-free, diabetic and so on. Over the years my sisters-in-law (one vegetarian and one diabetic), and recently my new step-daughter, who comes out in an itchy rash if she eats anything with gluten in it, have trained me to be more careful. These days I keep a stock of gluten-free ingredients. But here is a confession. I have never been able to produce decent pastry with gluten-free flour. Has anyone?

For all that I champion fresh, minimally processed food, you won't find anything about a clean gut and superfoods in here. I've included some good gluten-free and vegan recipes, but I'm the boring old granny who says there are no bad foods, but rather that anything in excess can kill you. Unless you have a serious health issue, a balanced diet will keep you well without any need for expensive supplements, unpleasant purges or miracle diets.

Cooking is not a religion. Friends are occasionally shocked that I will reach for the custard powder or packet of stock cubes, frozen mash or puff pastry, or that I seldom make my own bread. But I'm often in a hurry, so I'm for anything, however it's been arrived at, that works. For me, perfection means food that smells wonderful, looks wonderful, tastes wonderful and feels like heaven in the mouth. And, of course, it must be worth the calories!

Neat Tricks and Tips

Avocados

Rinse avocado chunks or slices under cold water to stop them browning – better than oil or lemon juice.

Pomegranates

To extract the seeds, use your hands to break apart the quartered fruit under water: the pith and skin float to the top, so are easy to skim off. The seeds will sink.

Freezing veg

Freeze fresh peas, sprouts or red summer fruits in a single layer on a baking tray lined with cling film. When frozen, bag them and they won't all stick together in a clump.

Bright greens

If pre-cooking green veg or blanching them for the freezer, cool them under cold water to keep the colour. Microwave or stir-fry to reheat.

Carrot ribbons

Use a peeler to cut peeled carrots into ribbons.

Frilly cucumbers

For frilly cucumber slices, score down the length of the cucumber with a fork, piercing the skin with the tips of the fork. Do this all round the cucumber, then slice.

Poaching eggs

If you struggle with the whirlpool method of poaching eggs, try using a wide, deep frying pan of simmering, salted water with a teaspoon of white vinegar in it. Slip the eggs in, side by side, and gently shake the pan by moving the handle from side to side to stop them catching on the bottom. They will come out flatter and less impressive than professionally poached eggs, but they'll taste just the same. For rounder eggs use a small, deep wok.

Lemon wedges

Here's how to cut the perfect lemon wedge that doesn't slip out of your fingers as you squeeze it, or drop pips on your food, or squirt your neighbour in the eye. First cut the lemon lengthways into six or eight wedges. Cut both ends squarely off each lemon wedge. Then cut along the thin edge of each wedge, to remove the pith and allow you to flick out the seeds.

Tomatoes

To peel a tomato, make a 1cm (½ in) nick in the skin with a sharp knife. Bring a pan of water to the boil, remove it from the heat and drop in the tomato. In about 10 seconds the skin will start to peel back where you made the nick and the tomato will be ready to peel. Cool it under cold water before peeling.

Pie fillings

Don't worry about preventing apple slices from browning when you're making a pie. Cooking gets them white again.

Wobbly boards

Put a folded damp cloth under your cutting board if it wobbles.

Cooling food

Cool food fast to prevent bugs breeding: spread it out in a shallow layer or stand the pot or bowl in cold water and stir occasionally. As soon as it's cool, refrigerate or freeze.

Freezing food

Freeze mash, stew, blanched veg or prepared pie fillings in a big bag and press flat – the thinner the better. They stack well in the freezer, you can break off bits as you need them, and they thaw much faster than they would in a big round lump.

I usually have raw homemade sausages in the freezer. I make lots, and freeze them on cling-film-lined baking trays. This way they don't stick to each other as they freeze. When frozen, I transfer them to plastic bags. If I want a few for supper I put them in a small sealed plastic bag and sink them in cold water, weighing them down if they want to float. They'll soften in 20 minutes or so.

Toasting nuts

To toast nuts, such as peeled almonds, put them in a frying pan without any fat and toss or turn them over medium heat until they are pale brown. Tip out immediately onto a plate. If you leave them in the pan they will continue to cook. If you are toasting masses of nuts, do them in a medium oven, spread out on a baking tray. But be very careful: after 5 minutes, check every minute and turn them sides to middle to stop some browning more quickly than others. Nuts can burn in a flash. I can't tell you how many I've lost that way over the years. Maddening and expensive!

Peeling garlic

Top and tail each clove and then bash it with the bottom of a jar or bottle. The skin will come off. Mash with a pinch of salt for a smooth paste.

Colouring pasta

Colour and flavour pasta by boiling it with a handful of kale leaves or slices of beetroot.

Crumble toppings

Add chopped nuts to sweet crumble toppings for extra crunch.

Pastry

Roll rich pastry out between two sheets of cling film. When rolled, remove the top sheet, then roll the pastry up with the bottom sheet, turn it over and unroll it onto the top of your flan tin or pie or whatever, removing the second sheet of cling film as you go.

Decorating cakes

If you want a smooth surface when frosting a cake, dip a palette knife into boiling hot water just before using.

Sift icing sugar over a less-than-lovely-looking cake or pastry.

To make chocolate leaves, paint holly leaves with melted chocolate, leave to set, then peel away the leaves. To make curls, pour melted chocolate onto a greased tray. Leave to set, then drag a cheese plane over the surface to create curls. If this is a fiddle, shop-bought Flake bars will often do the job. Or you could carefully scrape a veg peeler down the side of a chocolate bar to make shavings.

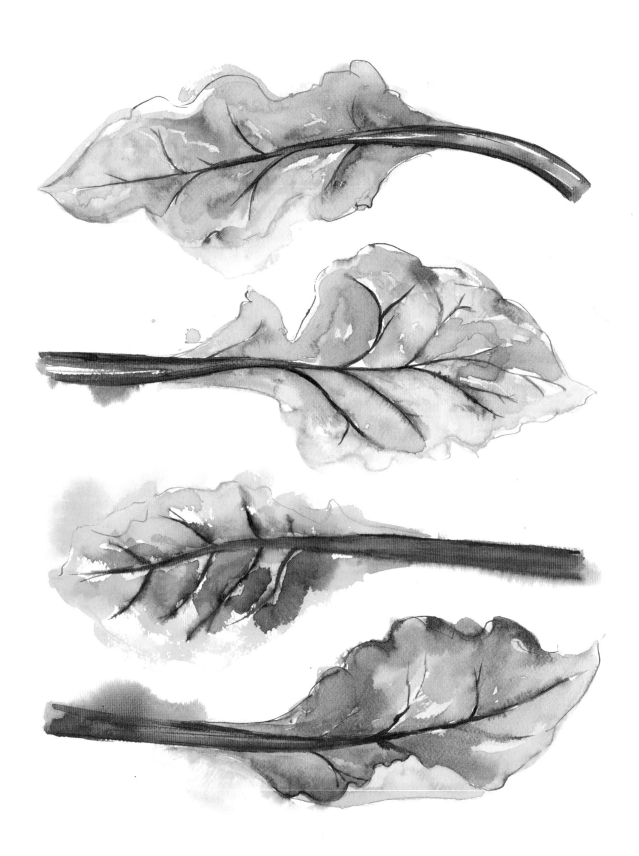

Simple Favourites

English summer pasta al pesto

Serves 6

600g tagliatelle

a little splash of olive oil

For the pesto

1 x 100g bunch
(or 3 packets) flat-leaf
parsley, stalks removed

140g fresh-as-possible
walnuts

3 large garlic cloves

170g mature Cheddar
cheese, broken into
2–3cm (1in) chunks

150ml rapeseed oil

salt and pepper to season

I first cooked this with my nephew Sam Leith, the journalist, during a photo shoot for *Saga magazine*. We made it up as we went along, and were both surprised at how delicious it was. The trick is to have really good walnuts, as fresh as possible – not the ones from the half-used pack at the back of the cupboard.

1. Heat a large saucepan of salted water over a medium heat. Once bubbling, add the tagliatelle and cook for 8–10 minutes (or 2–3 minutes for fresh pasta) until just al dente. Drain the pasta, rinse under hot water and leave in the colander to steam dry for a minute before returning to the pan. Stir through a little olive oil to prevent the pasta sticking together. Set aside.

2. While the pasta is cooking, make the pesto. Put the parsley, walnuts and garlic into a liquidizer or food processor and blitz till smooth. Then add the Cheddar and blitz some more. Gradually pour in the rapeseed oil as you continue to pulse until it looks like pesto.

3. Stir the pesto though the tagliatelle and serve immediately, seasoned with salt and pepper.

As with classic basil pesto, you can make the sauce a day or two in advance and keep it in the fridge or freezer. But after a day or so it begins to lose its marvellous vivid green. I prefer to have all the ingredients ready so I can easily make it while the pasta cooks.

Poached eggs on greens

1 tbsp olive oil

15g unsalted butter

1 small onion, finely sliced

1 garlic clove, finely crushed

a large handful of parsley leaves, finely chopped

200g broad beans

200g rainbow chard, leaves and stalks roughly chopped

200g baby spinach leaves

finely grated zest and juice of 1 small lemon

a good pinch of ground nutmeg

2 large eggs

a small handful of hazelnuts, toasted and roughly chopped

salt and pepper to season

After years of being labelled the bad-cholesterol villain, I'm glad to say that the humble egg has at last been given a clean bill of health, and we can now eat eggs without guilt. To be honest, I never stopped.

1. Heat the olive oil and butter in a large frying pan over a medium-low heat. Add the sliced onion, along with a good pinch of salt, and fry gently until soft and slightly golden. Add the garlic and parsley and cook for a further 2 minutes.

2. Meanwhile, bring a medium saucepan of water to the boil. Reduce the heat to a simmer and add the broad beans. Cook for 4–5 minutes, until just tender, before scooping out with a slotted spoon (you can reuse the water for poaching the eggs later). Rinse under cold water. Slip off the tough grey coats to reveal the bright green inner beans. Set aside.

3. Stir the chard and spinach into the softened onion mixture along with a tablespoon of water. Pile the leaves high, they will soon collapse as they cook. Cook for 5–7 minutes or until the greens have wilted. Stir though the beans, lemon zest and juice and nutmeg. Season with salt and pepper. Keep warm over a very low heat while you poach the eggs.

4. Set a saucepan of salted water over a high heat and bring to the boil. Crack one egg into a small cup or ramekin. Using a wooden spoon, rapidly swirl the water to make a whirlpool. Let the whirlpool almost completely subside before turning down to a simmer and gently tipping your egg into the centre of the whirlpool. Cook for 3 minutes. Remove with a slotted spoon and pat dry with kitchen paper. Repeat with the other egg.

5. Divide the wilted greens between two serving plates. Top each one with a soft poached egg, followed by a few hazelnuts. Finish with a little black pepper. Serve as is, or with crusty bread to mop up the juices.

If I have leftover greens I will toss them in a bit of butter (more cholesterol!) with plenty of garlic, then plonk poached eggs on top. You can vary the greens: leeks, sprouts and runner beans, or any combination of them, are all good.

Piedmont almond roasted peppers

Serves 4 as a main
or 8 as a starter

2 large red peppers

1 large yellow pepper

1 large Romano pepper

250g cherry tomatoes,
halved

8 tinned anchovy fillets

2 garlic cloves, finely sliced

80g whole blanched
(skinless) almonds

4 tbsp olive oil

a small handful of basil
leaves, torn

black pepper to season

I first saw something like this recipe in Delia's *Summer Cooking*, in the days when red peppers were still considered a bit exotic. Delia has always had a genius for being just ahead of the public, but not so out on a limb that they couldn't find the ingredients. The combination of peppers, tomatoes, olives and good olive oil is commonplace now, but it's still delicious, and the addition of anchovies gives a salty pop on the tongue, while the almonds add crunch and flavour. I like the mix of red, yellow and long Romano peppers, but if you can only get one kind, that's fine. Even green peppers will do – they just won't have the sweetness of the others.

1. Heat the oven to 160°C/fan 140°C/gas mark 3. Lightly grease an ovenproof serving dish.

2. Slice the peppers in half, splitting them from top to bottom and carefully cutting through the stalks too. Remove the seeds, leaving the stalks in place (these help the peppers to retain their shape during cooking) and lay the pepper halves, skin side down, in the prepared dish. Fill the cavities with the tomatoes. Slice the anchovy fillets in half lengthways and lay two halves atop each pepper. Divide the garlic slices and blanched almonds among the peppers.

3. Spoon ½ tablespoon olive oil over each pepper and season well with black pepper. Bake for about 50 minutes, until the flesh of the peppers has softened and the edges are beginning to char. Serve garnished with torn basil leaves.

> The addition of goat's cheese, chopped chilli or black olives – any or all – makes for good variations.

Avocado bruschetta

Serves 4

1 x 400g tin chickpeas, drained and rinsed

1½ tsp coriander seeds, crushed

1 tsp smoked paprika

1 tbsp extra virgin olive oil plus extra to drizzle

salt and pepper to season

For the guacamole

2 ripe avocados

2 small, ripe tomatoes, finely diced

2 spring onions, finely sliced

½ red chilli, deseeded and finely chopped

juice of ½ large lemon

a handful of coriander leaves, finely chopped, plus extra leaves to garnish

Posh breakfast cafes all serve avocado on toast these days, and it makes me wonder what took them so long. The Mexicans have been doing it for ever.

Avocado is good heated (but not really cooked) too. If I am trying to jolly-up leftovers or make a boring bit of chicken more interesting, I will toss chunks or thick slices of ripe avocado briefly in a non-stick pan and add it to the dish. Good with almost anything: lamb, mince, stew or vegetarian casseroles. If you like this idea, try the Colombian Chicken and Potato Soup on page 156.

1. Heat the oven to 180°C/fan 160°C/gas mark 4.

2. Pat the chickpeas dry with kitchen paper, so they will crisp up more quickly in the oven. Place in a mixing bowl and toss together with the coriander seeds, paprika, olive oil and a good pinch of salt. Spread out on a baking tray and roast in the oven for 25 minutes, shaking them a little at the halfway point. When the chickpeas are ready, they should be a deep golden colour and crunchy all the way through to the centre. Set aside to cool completely.

3. For the guacamole, peel the avocados, removing the stones. Put the flesh into a bowl. Smash with a wooden spoon, leaving the consistency chunky. Add the tomatoes, spring onions, chilli, lemon juice and chopped coriander. Gently combine, then season with salt and pepper to taste.

4. Toast the sourdough. Divide the slices between four plates and top each slice with a mound of guacamole. Just before serving, top with the crunchy chickpeas, an extra drizzle of olive oil and some coriander leaves.

Black rice kedgeree

2 tbsp sunflower oil

a knob of butter

2 onions, finely sliced

1 large garlic clove, crushed

1 cinnamon stick

8 dried curry leaves

1 tsp ground turmeric

2 tsp medium curry powder

1 tsp black mustard seeds

300g black rice

600ml chicken stock

200g undyed smoked
haddock, skinned

2 x 100g salmon fillets

300ml milk

1 bay leaf

4 medium eggs

½ small bunch parsley,
leaves picked and
roughly chopped

½ small green chilli,
finely sliced

salt and pepper to season

I first learnt to make kedgeree when I started my catering business. Posh English clients, whose hunt balls or children's twenty-first-birthday dances I would be cooking for, would want something stodgy to soak up all the beer at about two in the morning.

I'm sure a top-notch Indian chef would shudder, but ever since the time of the British Raj, when the English co-opted, altered and bastardized traditional Indian dishes, kedgeree has appeared on our breakfast or supper tables. And with good reason. It's just delicious, especially with the dramatic-looking and great-tasting black rice.

1. Begin with a large shallow pan on a medium heat. Add the oil and butter, along with the onions and a good pinch of salt. Fry the onions, stirring often, until softened and golden brown – about 10 minutes. Add the garlic, cinnamon stick, curry leaves, turmeric, curry powder and mustard seeds and cook for a couple of minutes. Add the rice and chicken stock and stir once to prevent the rice from sticking. Cover with a close-fitting lid, reduce the heat to low and leave to cook gently for 45 minutes or until tender. Turn off the heat, but leave the lid on and allow the rice to steam in its own heat for a further 10 minutes.

2. Meanwhile, put the haddock and salmon in a saucepan with the milk and bay leaf. Simmer gently for 4 minutes before turning off the heat and allowing the fish to cool slowly in the milk; it will continue to cook in the residual heat. Once it's cool enough to handle, discard the milk and bay leaf and gently flake the cooked fish, discarding any skin or bones.

3. Bring a large saucepan of lightly salted water to the boil. Add the eggs to the pan and simmer for 7 minutes. Remove with a slotted spoon and transfer to a bowl of cold water to cool. Peel the eggs and cut in half.

4. Strain off any remaining stock from the rice and season to taste. Using a light touch, and a fork rather than a wooden spoon, 'stir' through almost all of the flaked fish and most of the parsley. Take care not to damage the flakes of fish – it only requires two or three 'stirs'. Return to the heat for a moment to warm, before transferring to a large, warm dish. Serve, topped with the eggs, chilli, reserved fish and parsley.

Almost a Thai fish cake

300g floury potatoes, peeled

1 medium egg, beaten

3 tbsp coriander leaves
and stalks, finely chopped

½ green chilli, finely
chopped

300g salmon fillet,
skinned and cut into
1–2cm (½ in) cubes

3cm (1in) piece of ginger,
peeled and finely grated

finely grated zest of 1 lime

1 lemongrass stem

3–4 tbsp dried breadcrumbs

2 tbsp sesame oil

1 tbsp unsalted butter

salt and pepper to season

For the dipping sauce

4 tbsp rice wine vinegar

1 tbsp mirin

2 tbsp Thai fish sauce
(nam pla)

juice of 1 lime

1 tsp honey

½ red chilli, deseeded
and very finely chopped

Little Thai fish cakes – as sold on the streets of Bangkok – are almost always delicious, usually made with no potato and a lot of chilli, but here I have combined the South East Asian flavours of lemongrass, coriander and chilli with English potatoes.

1. Bring a large saucepan of salted water to the boil, add the potatoes and simmer until tender, about 20 minutes. Drain well, and while still boiling-hot, crush (rather than mash) the potatoes and allow the steam to escape – the drier the mash, the firmer your fish cakes will be. Leave the mash to cool before stirring in the egg, coriander and green chilli. Generously season with salt and pepper. Set aside.

2. While the potatoes are cooking, whizz the salmon, ginger and lime zest in a food processor until they form a thick paste.

3. Peel the outer layer of the lemongrass and discard. Cut the stem in half lengthways and chop as finely as you are able. Add to the salmon paste, then add the salmon mixture to the cooled potato, combining well. Divide the mixture into eight and shape into patties. Dip each one into the breadcrumbs to coat and put onto a large plate or baking tray. Chill in the fridge for at least an hour to firm up the fishcakes.

4. Place a large, heavy-based frying pan over a medium heat. Heat the sesame oil and butter together in the pan until beginning to foam, then fry the fish cakes in batches, until golden on both sides.

5. To make the dipping sauce, combine all the ingredients and pour into a small serving dish. Serve the hot fish cakes with the dipping sauce.

> You can buy very good lemongrass paste and ginger paste in tubes and keep them in the fridge. These save a lot of bother and are almost (but not quite) as good!
>
> Sometimes I use quarters of fresh lime or a not-too-sweet chilli sauce instead of the dipping sauce.

Chard, bacon
and fried potato frittata

Serves 6

400g floury potatoes,
peeled and cut into
4cm (1½ in) chunks

a good knob
of unsalted butter

2 tbsp olive oil

150g rainbow chard, stalks
trimmed, roughly chopped,
plus 50g extra, with stalks
trimmed but left whole

3 banana shallots, peeled
and quartered

100g smoked bacon lardons

6 large eggs

60ml whole milk
or double cream

½ tbsp wholegrain mustard

60g strong Cheddar
cheese, grated

salt and pepper to season

You can't make a frittata successfully without finishing it in the oven. Believe me, I've tried when I'm in a hurry, or feeling too mean to turn on my great big oven for such a little pan. But the thing is, as a good frittata is quite thick, like a tray-bake, the bottom will be scorched before you've fried it long enough to set the egg. And anyway, you won't have a cheesy brown top. If you're in a rush, it's better to make individual thin omelettes, rather than a family-sized frittata.

1. Bring a large saucepan of salted water to the boil and cook the potatoes for 7–10 minutes or until just tender but not falling apart. Drain and leave to steam dry in the colander or sieve for 5 minutes.

2. In a large, heavy-based ovenproof frying pan, melt half the butter with half the olive oil over a medium-low heat. Add the potatoes and fry, turning gently every so often, until golden brown and beginning to crisp up. Remove from the pan, season with salt and set aside.

3. Bring a large saucepan of lightly salted water to the boil. Add the chard and blanch for 4 minutes. Drain and plunge the cooked chard into cold water. Drain thoroughly, then set aside.

4. Heat the oven to 160°C/fan 140°C/gas mark 3.

5. Go back to the frying pan. Melt the remaining butter and oil in the pan over a medium heat. Add the shallots and lardons and fry for 10 minutes or until the shallots have softened and the lardons are turning golden brown.

6. In a large mixing bowl, gently combine the eggs, milk or cream, mustard and half the Cheddar. Season with salt and pepper to taste.

7. Stir the fried potatoes and the chopped chard into the shallot and bacon mixture. Pour in the egg mixture and cook over a medium heat for 5 minutes or until the bottom has just set. Lay the whole chard leaves on top and sprinkle over the remaining cheese, then transfer the frittata to the oven and cook for a further 10–15 minutes or until gently set, with a slight wobble in the centre. Cut into wedges and serve with a bitter salad.

Penne with aubergine and garlic

Serves 4

2 large aubergines

400g dried penne

2 tbsp olive oil

a knob of salted butter

a small handful of flat-leaf parsley leaves and stalks, finely chopped

3 garlic cloves, crushed

finely grated zest and juice of 1 large lemon

½ tsp dried chilli flakes

a handful of squishy black olives, pitted

75g ricotta salata or Parmesan, shaved

salt and pepper to season

Hearty, aromatic and filling, this pasta dish is delicious served with a simple salad of sliced ripe tomatoes and finely chopped red onion, dressed with a little balsamic glaze, salt and pepper.

1. Pierce the aubergines twice with a sharp knife to prevent them exploding in the oven.

2. If you have a combined oven and grill, heat the oven to its hottest setting and, once roasting hot, turn it to the grill setting. Place the aubergines on a baking sheet under the grill, with the oven door closed, for 20 minutes, turning halfway through, or until the skin is black and the flesh is collapsed and soft. If using a gas grill, grill the aubergines under a high heat, turning frequently.

3. Meanwhile, bring a large saucepan of salted water to the boil, add the penne and cook for 11 minutes or until al dente. Drain the pasta and allow to steam dry in the colander for a minute before returning to the pan. Stir in the olive oil to prevent the pasta sticking together.

4. Slice the hot aubergines lengthways to reveal the soft flesh, being careful not to cut all the way through. Once the steam has disappeared, spoon the buttery flesh into a bowl. Stir through the butter, parsley, garlic, lemon zest and juice and chilli flakes. Season generously.

5. Mix the penne and soft aubergine, then stir through the olives. Serve with shavings of ricotta salata or Parmesan.

If you bake the aubergines more slowly, the skin will not be charred to a crisp and you can chop the whole lot up, skin and all to make a more rustic version of the dish.

Baked angel-hair pasta with rich tomato sauce

Serves 4

For the tomato sauce

3 tbsp olive oil

2 onions, finely sliced

2 large garlic cloves, chopped

1 red chilli, deseeded and finely chopped

½ tsp fennel seeds

2 tsp ground coriander

4 tbsp tomato purée

2 x 400g tins good-quality chopped tomatoes

a pinch of salt

1 tbsp soft brown sugar

1 tbsp parsley leaves, coarsely chopped

For the bake

3 tbsp olive oil

300g capellini pasta (angel-hair spaghetti)

450ml hot vegetable stock

To serve

green salad

garlic-flavoured mayonnaise

This is a surprising dish, invented by Leith's School of Food and Wine. The pasta underneath is moist, while that at the top is delightfully crunchy. You can doctor bought mayonnaise if you don't want to make your own – just add crushed garlic and lemon juice to a jar of (preferably) olive oil mayonnaise.

And, yes, I know: there's a lot of oil in this recipe. But it's really good!

1. Start by making the tomato sauce: heat the oil in a frying pan, over a medium heat. Add the onions and soften over a gentle heat for 5–6 minutes. Add the garlic, chilli and dried spices, and continue to cook, stirring, for a couple more minutes. Add the tomato purée. Pour in the tinned tomatoes, season with salt and add the sugar. Stir well and then simmer very gently, uncovered, for about 30 minutes or until the sauce is lovely and thick. Stir through the parsley.

2. For the bake, heat the oven to 200°C/fan 180°C/gas mark 6. Pour the olive oil into the biggest frying pan you have and set over a medium heat. Scrunch the pasta nests in your hands to break the strands. Fry the pasta, in batches, in the hot oil, turning until it is an even pale brown (it will get browner in the oven). Drain on kitchen paper. Tip any remaining oil out of the pan, and return the pasta to it, along with the tomato sauce and the stock. Stir over the heat for a minute or two before tipping into a 2-litre ovenproof dish.

3. Bake, uncovered, for 20–25 minutes in the middle of the oven – by which time the sauce should be reduced, and the pasta should be crisp and brown on top and soft underneath. The top may catch slightly, but that's fine. Serve with a fresh, leafy salad and garlic mayonnaise.

> If freezing the pasta bake for later, cook until the end of Step 2. Cool it at this point, cover and freeze. Thaw before proceeding, and don't forget to preheat the oven.

Blood orange
and blue cheese salad

Serves 6

3 blood oranges

2 heads of chicory
(red or white)

a handful of flat-leaf parsley
leaves, roughly chopped

150g blue cheese, cut into
rough chunks

For the vinaigrette

1 tbsp white wine vinegar

3 tbsp olive oil

½ tsp honey

½ tsp Dijon mustard

salt and pepper to season

Blue cheese and orange is a marriage made in heaven, and any slightly bitter leaves, such as endive or chicory, sets them off a treat. For me, the best is Belgian endive (the bullet-shaped white or purple-edged one, confusingly sold as white or red chicory), with its smooth crisp leaves. It can also stand being dressed a few hours in advance.

1. Peel the oranges: cut a slice from the top and bottom thick enough to remove both skin and pith, then hold the orange on a board and, with a sharp serrated knife, cut skin and pith off together with downward strokes, trying not to squeeze with your steadying hand. Work around the orange, then turn it over and trim off any remaining skin. Repeat with the other oranges. Then cut them all across into thin slices.

2. Put the vinaigrette ingredients into a big bowl and whisk until smooth and combined.

3. Break the individual leaves from the chicory and add them to the bowl. Add the parsley, and then turn gently to coat each leaf. Divide between six plates.

4. Top each salad with orange slices and cheese. Season with a little salt and black pepper, then serve.

> Single chicory leaves filled with teaspoons of blue cheese and tiny segments of any citrus fruit make great party bites.
>
> Try this salad with fresh pears or any other citrus (pomelo, pink grapefruit, clementines). If they aren't sweet enough, you may need a touch more honey in the dressing.

Prue's easy party pasta

Serves 6–8

350g pasta shells, macaroni pieces or tagliatelle

a dash of olive oil

2 onions, finely sliced

a large knob of butter

225g chestnut mushrooms, sliced

2 garlic cloves, crushed

15 or so ripe cherry tomatoes, cut into quarters

80g finely sliced ham, torn or cut into smaller strips

75g mature Cheddar cheese, finely grated

a good handful of chives or spring onion tops, chopped

salt and pepper to season

This is cooking at its absolute simplest and easiest, using standard ingredients. It's delicious, it doesn't cost much and children like it, so you don't have to cook something separate for fussy kids. And you can vary the ingredients depending on what you have in the fridge – the quantities are only a rough guide.

1. Bring a large saucepan of salted water to a gentle simmer. Add the pasta and cook for 8–9 minutes or until just al dente. Drain well and rinse off any excess starch under hot running water. Return the cooked pasta to the pan and toss in just enough oil to stop it sticking together.

2. In a heavy-based frying pan, gently cook the onions in the butter until they are soft and translucent, then add the mushrooms and continue cooking for a further minute or two. Add the garlic and finally the tomatoes and ham. Shake the pan over the heat until everything is hot. With a fork, mix the contents of the frying pan into the hot pasta and stir through the grated cheese and the chives. Season with salt and pepper.

3. Turn out into a hot dish and serve immediately, perhaps with a fresh green salad.

> This dish is very forgiving. You can reheat it, covered, in the oven or microwave – but add the cheese and chives just before serving.

Toasted couscous salad
with chicken tikka

Serves 8

250g couscous

250ml chicken stock

a glug of olive oil

1 large onion, finely sliced

4 garlic cloves, finely sliced

1 tsp ground cumin

4 chicken breasts, sliced into thin strips

4 generous tbsp tikka paste

1 lemon

200g sun-dried tomatoes, cut into quarters

salt and pepper to season

For the salad

½ cucumber

1 large, ripe avocado, peeled and cut into 2cm (¾ in) chunks

300g cherry tomatoes, halved

80g baby spinach leaves

I begged this recipe from an old friend. It's as easy as pie to do (actually it's a whole heap easier than pie, which isn't necessarily easy at all) and makes a pretty and unusual main dish for lunch, is popular on a buffet table, and can be prepared in advance.

1. Start by preparing the couscous: heat a large non-stick frying pan over a medium heat. Add the couscous to the pan and toast gently for 5–7 minutes or until the grains are a toasted, golden brown colour, shaking the pan occasionally. Tip into a large heatproof bowl.

2. Heat the stock to boiling point and pour over the couscous. Fluff up with a fork, then cover with a plate or baking tray and leave for 10 minutes until all the liquid is nicely absorbed. Set aside.

3. Wipe the frying pan clean, add the olive oil and return the pan to a medium-high heat. Add the onion and fry until soft and brown, but by no means burnt, about 4–5 minutes. Add the garlic and cumin to the pan and cook, stirring, over a lower heat for a further minute. Stir in the chicken strips and tikka paste and cook gently for 10–12 minutes, until the chicken is cooked through. Remove from the heat and allow to cool slightly.

4. Meanwhile, prepare the salad. Slice the cucumber lengthways and, using a teaspoon, scrape the seeds from the middle. Discard the seeds and slice the flesh into thin crescents. Tip into a large mixing bowl and use a fork to gently toss together with the avocado, tomatoes and spinach leaves. Arrange the salad around the edge of a large serving plate.

5. Use a lemon zester or fine potato peeler to remove the outer yellow zest of the lemon, taking care not to take any pith. If using a peeler, cut the strips of zest into fine matchsticks. Squeeze the juice.

6. Now, back to the couscous: lightly fork the sun-dried tomatoes through the warm couscous. Still using a fork, lightly mix in the chicken tikka mixture too – be careful not to over-mix which could glue everything together. Tip or spoon the couscous into the centre of your plate, scatter over the lemon zest and juice and season with salt and pepper.

The real quiche Lorraine

For the pastry

180g plain flour

a pinch of salt

100g cold unsalted butter, chopped

1 medium egg

For the filling

1 tbsp butter

1 small onion, finely chopped

100g streaky bacon, diced

150ml milk

150ml single cream

3 medium eggs, beaten

75g strong Cheddar or Gruyère cheese, grated

salt and pepper to season

When Caroline Waldegrave and I opened Leith's School of Food and Wine in 1975, we used to teach this in the first lesson, along with *coq au vin* and *mousse au chocolat*. They might sound posh but are not difficult to make, and they taught the beginner a lot: this recipe gave them pastry, lining a flan ring, chopping onions, baking custard. The results, if not award-winning, always tasted good. So here is the classic, no-nonsense but utterly delicious, quiche Lorraine.

1. Sift the flour and salt into a large bowl. Rub in the butter until the mixture resembles coarse breadcrumbs. In a separate bowl, mix the egg with 2–3 tablespoons of very cold water and sprinkle half over the flour – it may be necessary to add more liquid, but the pastry should not be too damp. Mix to a firm dough, first with a knife, and finally with one hand. Gather the pastry to form a rough square.

2. Roll out the pastry on a lightly floured surface and use to line a 24cm (9in) flan ring or loose-bottomed flan tin, pressing it gently into the corners. Trim the edge level with the top of the tin. Chill for 30 minutes.

3. Heat the oven to 180°C/fan 160°C/gas mark 4. Line the pastry case with baking parchment and fill it with dried beans, rice or ceramic baking beans. Bake the pastry in the top third of the oven for 20 minutes or until the pastry is sandy-coloured. Remove the baking beans and paper and return the case to the oven for a further 8–10 minutes. Leave to cool. Reduce the oven temperature to 150°C/fan 130°C/gas mark 2.

4. For the filling, melt the butter in a frying pan over a medium-low heat. Add the onion and bacon and fry gently, until the onion is soft but not coloured. Leave to cool.

5. Mix together the milk, cream and eggs, then add the onion, bacon and cheese. Season with salt and pepper if needed.

6. Pour the mixture into the flan case and bake in the centre of the oven for about 40 minutes or until the filling has set firm but barely browned. Carefully remove the flan ring and bake the quiche for a further 5–10 minutes to allow the pastry to brown a little. Serve warm or cold.

Braised duck salad with pomegranate, juniper and ginger

(Pictured overleaf.)

Serves 6

5 celery sticks, finely diced

1 large red onion,
finely chopped

6 garlic cloves, crushed

6cm (2½ in) piece of ginger,
peeled and finely chopped

2 tsp juniper berries (see
Tip opposite)

juice and finely grated zest
of 1 orange

a glug of vegetable oil

2 tsp za'atar (see Tip
opposite)

4 duck legs, skin on

1 large pomegranate

1 bunch of spring onions,
finely sliced on the diagonal

salt and pepper to season

For the dressing

juice of ½ lemon

2 tbsp pomegranate
molasses (see Tip opposite)

2 tbsp extra virgin olive oil

I once saw Jamie Oliver do something like this (though I never managed to get the recipe) years ago at a Good Food Show. The audience consisted of 2,000 schoolchildren and even before he appeared they were pretty hysterical, shouting 'Jamie, Jamie!' at the top of their lungs while music pounded and the word JAMIE pulsed in neon colours. There was a huge drum kit on one side of the stage and he leapt onto the stool and played a riff with all the expertise of a rock star. Then he came centre stage and gave a cookery demonstration, involving kids from the audience at every step, with two of them shredding the duck, others chopping, peeling etc. I remember his trick with the pomegranate: instead of following my method below, he bashed the fruit all over (like you might tap a hard-boiled egg to make peeling it easy), then cut it in half and squeezed the fruit in his fists, holding them high over the bowl. The seeds and juice rained down on the salad.

1. Heat the oven to 180°C/fan 160°C/gas mark 4.

2. Put the celery, onion, garlic and ginger in the bottom of a shallow casserole dish. Bash the juniper berries lightly in a small pestle and mortar (or in a bowl with the end of a rolling pin) and add them to the casserole. Add the orange juice and zest and drizzle with a good glug of vegetable oil. Give it a good mix and spread out to make a bed for the duck legs.

3. Rub the za'atar all over the duck legs and lay them on top of the vegetables in the casserole. Season well with salt and pepper. Now simply place in the oven and cook, uncovered, for roughly 1½ hours, depending on the size of your duck legs. The duck is done when the flesh easily pulls away from the bone with the touch of a fork.

4. Meanwhile, remove the seeds from the pomegranate. The best method for this is to score the tough outer skin into quarters. Submerge the fruit in a large, deep bowl of cold water and, using your hands, gently pull apart the quarters and ease out the seeds with your fingers. The seeds sink to the bottom and the skin and pith will float to the top and can be scooped away. Drain off the water and the seeds remain. (Don't leave the seeds in the water too long – tip them out onto kitchen paper to dry.)

5. Remove the duck from the oven. Pour off the duck fat from the vegetables. Allow the duck to cool for a few minutes to make removing the meat from the bones easier.

6. Shred the duck and skin and tip into a large mixing bowl. Tumble together with the roasted vegetables and then turn out onto a generous serving platter.

7. Make the dressing by combining the lemon juice, pomegranate molasses and olive oil.

8. Serve before the duck cools completely: drizzle the dressing all over, then top with the pomegranate seeds and sliced spring onions.

Some of these ingredients, such as juniper berries, za'atar (a Middle Eastern herb and spice mix) and pomegranate molasses, are only available in the biggest of supermarkets or in specialist stores. But they are all available online, are worth the effort, and can be used in other dishes. I like juniper in all sorts of pork recipes, za'atar as a rub for grilled meats and to give boring carbs a boost, and pomegranate molasses makes a change from balsamic dressing in salads.

Homemade sausages
with tomato sauce

Serves 4 adults
or 6 children

For the tomato sauce

3 tbsp olive oil

2 onions, sliced

2 large garlic cloves,
chopped

2 tsp ground coriander

4 tbsp tomato purée

2 x 400g tins good-quality
chopped tomatoes

a pinch of salt

1½ tsp soft brown sugar

1 tbsp parsley leaves,
coarsely chopped

For the sausages

800g pork shoulder, minced

80g dried breadcrumbs

1 tsp salt

a good grating of black
pepper

2 tbsp parsley leaves,
chopped

sausage skins (optional)

1 tbsp cooking oil for
greasing

As with the meatballs on page 176, experimentation is fun here. Any minced meat, flavoured as you like, can be used, and there's no need to stuff them into sausage skins, which I only used to do when I had an old Kenwood mixer that boasted a sausage-filling attachment. Now I just wet my hands and roll the mixture into sausage shapes. If they look a bit homemade and rustic, so much the better.

1. Start by making the tomato sauce: heat the oil in a frying pan, over a medium heat. Add the onions and soften over a gentle heat for 5 minutes.

2. Add the garlic and coriander and continue to cook, stirring, for a couple more minutes. Add the tomato purée and tinned tomatoes, season with salt and add the sugar. Stir well.

3. Simmer gently, uncovered, for about 30 minutes or until the sauce is lovely and thick. Stir in the parsley.

4. Heat the oven to 180°C/fan 160°C/gas mark 4.

5. For the sausages, put all the ingredients except the sausage skins and oil in a bowl and mix well with your hands, adjusting the seasoning to taste (see Tip below). Then divide the mixture into eight portions and shape into sausages, or stuff the mixture into sausage skins, twisting the skin between each 10cm (4in) length to divide into sausages, then cut through each link to separate them.

6. Put the sausages into a roasting tin with the oil and carefully turn them to grease them all over.

7. Bake the sausages for 20 minutes, turning them once halfway through, until golden and slightly charred in places. Remove the sausages from the oven and drain off any runaway fat. Tip the tomato sauce into a medium-sized ovenproof dish, arrange the sausages on top and bake for a further 5–8 minutes. Serve.

> If you don't want to taste your sausagemeat raw at Step 5, fry a teaspoon of it, then taste and adjust the seasoning.

Celariac remoulade with tarragon and salami

Serves 4

For the mayonnaise

2 medium egg yolks

1 tbsp Dijon mustard

200ml light olive oil

3 tbsp lemon juice

salt and pepper to season

For the salad

1 small celeriac

100g salami, sliced into very thin strips

a small handful of tarragon leaves, chopped

1 lemon, cut into wedges to serve

This is a classic celeriac remoulade, but gingered up with a bit of spicy salami. Any will do, but for this dish I prefer a large moist Italian salami to the very hard French saucisson. Of course you could use bottled mayo – but honestly, this is one dish where the effort of making the real thing is absolutely worth it. Serve with toast as a light supper dish, as a light lunch with a poached egg on top or as a salad on a buffet.

1. Begin by making proper mayonnaise for your dressing. Using a wooden spoon or small hand whisk, beat the egg yolks and mustard together in a medium-sized bowl. Slowly add the oil, at first almost drip by drip, certainly not faster than the thinnest stream, constantly beating as you do so. The mixture will gradually become thick and creamy. A liquidizer or food processor will do the job too. Just remember to add the oil very gradually at first, getting bolder as it thickens. When all the oil is in, stir in the lemon juice and 1 tablespoon of cold water. Taste, and season well.

2. For the salad, peel the celeriac and slice the flesh into the thinnest of slices, as thin as your knife skills allow. Then stack the slices and cut them into thin strips. Alternatively, if you have a food processor, put chunks of celeriac through the coarse grater or julienne cutter. Mix with the mustardy mayonnaise and salami and add the tarragon. Season to taste, adding a good few turns of the pepper mill, but going easy on the salt because the salami will be salty.

3. Serve the remoulade with lemon wedges.

If your mayonnaise curdles, it's because you added too much oil at once or didn't whisk with enough wellie, I'm afraid. You'll just have to start again with another couple of egg yolks and gradually beat in the split mixture and then add more oil to make twice as much mayo as you need! The leftover mayo will keep in the fridge for a few days, though.

Warm sweet potato, pak choi and feta salad

Serves 6

1.25kg small sweet potatoes, peeled and each cut into 8 long wedges

3 tbsp olive oil

1 tsp smoked paprika

2 small pak choi or 3.5cm (1½ in) large Chinese cabbage

100g feta, crumbled

a handful of coriander leaves, roughly chopped

1 tbsp toasted sesame seeds to serve

For the dressing

2 tsp finely grated ginger

1 small garlic clove, crushed

1 red or green chilli, deseeded and finely chopped

2 tbsp light soy sauce

2 tbsp toasted sesame oil

3 tbsp groundnut oil

salt and pepper to season

I grew up in South Africa, where I got to love sweetish carbs like pumpkin, corn-on-the-cob, butternut and sweet potato. This salad combines the earthy smokiness of griddled sweet potato, familiar to me from childhood barbecues, with a later love of Far Eastern flavours of ginger, chilli and soy. Pak choi (or bok choy) is available as a big white Chinese cabbage, or as small greener plants, usually served in stir-fries. I think the small ones have slightly more flavour but, to be honest, neither have much – you could just as well use English white cabbage.

1. Heat the oven to 200°C/fan 180°C/gas mark 6. Grease a baking tray (or line it with baking parchment).

2. Brush the sweet potato wedges with olive oil to coat them all over and season generously with salt. Heat a griddle pan until smoking hot and put the sweet potato wedges straight onto the griddle. Don't overcrowd the pan (this can lead to steaming, rather than grilling). Give the wedges 3–4 minutes to char before turning them over and griddling the other side for a few minutes. (Resist the urge to move them – the griddle lines will only appear if the wedges are left to carbonize.)

3. Allow to cool slightly, then tip them onto the prepared baking tray, sprinkle over the smoked paprika and cook in the centre of the oven for 10–12 minutes, or until they are soft and cooked through.

4. Slice the pak choi leaves and put into a large mixing bowl with the warm sweet potato, feta and coriander.

5. Mix together the dressing ingredients and pour into the bowl. Use your hands to combine everything very gently. Transfer to a large serving plate and sprinkle with the sesame seeds.

You could use plain sesame oil, but toast the sesame seeds if you do this – shake them in a dry pan over high heat until pale brown.

If time is short, omit the griddling of the sweet potato wedges. The salad will still work well without the charred flavour, just be sure to cook the wedges in the oven for a little longer, until they are crisp.

Family fish pie

(Pictured overleaf.)

I've eaten a lot of fish pie in my life (what mum and grandmother hasn't?) but I still think this one is the best for flavour, for freezing and for popularity with everyone. I first learnt how to make it at cooking school fifty-six years ago! This method uses 50% cornflour and 50% plain flour to thicken the sauce, which is perfect for freezing. Plain flour gives the sauce a better texture but doesn't defrost as well.

Serves 6

1kg Maris Piper potatoes, peeled and halved or quartered

50–75ml semi-skimmed milk

a knob of butter

For the filling

300ml semi-skimmed or whole milk

¼ onion, sliced

4 black peppercorns

1 bay leaf

200g salmon fillet, cut into bite-sized chunks

400g haddock fillet, cut into bite-sized chunks

5 medium eggs, hard-boiled

30g butter

2 heaped tsp plain flour

2 heaped tsp cornflour

2 tbsp double cream

a small handful of flat-leaf parsley, roughly chopped

finely grated zest of 1 small lemon

salt and pepper to season

1. Firstly, make your mash. Cook the potatoes in salted boiling water for about 15 minutes until they are tender and cut like soft butter. Drain well and return to the pan, cover, then shake well so the potatoes break up a little. Remove the lid and allow them to steam dry for a minute or two. Mash with the milk, butter and plenty of salt and pepper, until smooth and fluffy. Set aside to get cold.

2. Heat the oven to 180°C/fan 160°C/gas mark 4.

3. For the filling, put the milk, onion, peppercorns, bay leaf and a pinch of salt in a small saucepan and heat until steaming. Remove from the heat and set aside for 3–4 minutes to infuse and cool slightly. Lay the salmon and haddock in a small roasting tin, skin side down. Strain the infused milk over the fish, discarding the flavourings. Cover with a lid or foil and bake in the oven for 10–12 minutes, until the fish is barely cooked through, just enough to feel firm and for the skin to peel off easily. Strain the milk (reserving it for later) and transfer the fish to a large bowl. Remove any bones and the skin.

4. Peel the eggs and cut lengthways into quarters.

5. Melt the butter in a medium saucepan, stir in the plain flour and cook for a minute. Remove from the heat. In a jug or large cup, mix the cornflour with a little of the reserved milk until smooth, then stir in half of the remaining milk. Now add this to the butter and flour in the pan, a little at a time, stirring to avoid lumps. Return the pan to the heat, add the remaining milk and bring to the boil, stirring. Reduce the heat and simmer for 2 minutes. Add the double cream, parsley and lemon zest.

6. Lay the fish in a 2-litre pie dish, along with the egg quarters. Pour over the sauce.

7. Spoon a layer of mash over the fish, starting from the edges. Once the filling is covered, create a criss-cross pattern on the top using the back of a fork. Put the pie on a baking tray and bake in the oven until the top is just beginning to brown – about 30 minutes.

There are all sorts of delicious variations on fish pie: smoked fish is good; chopped tarragon makes a sophisticated addition (though I find 'green bits' can put my grandchildren off); cooked peas, mushrooms or broccoli can stretch the pie. Sometimes I like to add curry paste to the sauce. It's a great dish for experimentation.

Cambodian crab salad

½ cucumber, deseeded and cut into 1–1.5cm (½ in) dice

200g radishes, finely sliced

¼ cantaloupe melon (about 300g), deseeded and cut into 1–1.5cm (½ in) dice

½ papaya, deseeded and cut into 1–1.5cm (½ in) dice

200g white crabmeat

160g cooked prawns

a good fistful of mint leaves, finely chopped

salt and pepper to season

For the dressing

1 lemongrass stem

5cm (2in) piece of ginger

finely grated zest and juice of 1 lime

2 tbsp Thai fish sauce (nam pla)

To serve

40g coconut flakes

1 tbsp dried prawn powder or crushed dried shrimp

handful of fresh pomegranate seeds

My daughter Li-Da is Cambodian, and one of her Cambodian friends taught us both how to make this salad. And then later, when we were staying in Koh Samui, we had a cookery lesson and learnt the Thai version. I've eaten something similar in Vietnam too, so I conclude you can do what you like. But what stays the same is the dressing, although even there you might use hoisin sauce for meat versions and nam pla (fish sauce) for seafood or fish ones. The main thing is to chop everything finely, and ensure that you have the basic elements of protein (tuna, seafood, smoked salmon, chicken, duck), salad (always cucumber, radishes and mint but sometimes chicory, Gem lettuce or rocket) and some sweet fruit (melon, pomegranate, papaya, pineapple or mango).

1. Not more than 4 hours ahead of serving, prepare the cucumber, radishes, melon and papaya, slicing and dicing them as finely as you can. Gently combine the cucumber, radishes, melon and papaya in a large bowl.

2. To make the dressing, remove and discard the outer layers of the lemongrass, bash the rest with a rolling pin, and then slice it as finely as possible. Peel the ginger (I find a teaspoon pushed under the skin helps) and grate or chop finely, then put the lemongrass and ginger in a screw-top jar with the rest of the dressing ingredients and shake well.

3. Toast the coconut flakes in a dry frying pan over a medium heat, gently tossing them until golden. They burn easily, so keep watch.

4. Just before serving, add the crabmeat, prawns and mint to the salad. Toss together with the dressing, taste and season, then serve sprinkled with the coconut flakes, prawn powder and pomegranate seeds.

Dried shrimp or prawn powder is available in Asian shops or online. It makes a big difference to the flavour, so it's worth the trouble to find it.

Tuna, green bean and wasabi salad

Serves 4

200g green beans

300g frozen edamame beans

1 ripe avocado

vegetable oil for deep-frying

40g vermicelli or thin
rice noodles

4 thick tuna steaks
(about 150g each and
1.5cm/¾ in thick)

olive oil for coating

salt and pepper to season

pickled ginger to serve

For the wasabi dressing

3 Thai shallots or 1 banana
shallot, finely sliced

juice of 1 lime

2 tbsp sesame oil (preferably
toasted)

1 tbsp rice wine vinegar

1 tsp wasabi paste

This is a great tuna salad, excellent cooked-and-eaten-at-once so it is still warm for a few people, or served cold for a crowd. I've served it cold and in small portions (without the noodles) for a summer dinner-party starter too.

It's important to keep the tuna rare in the middle, so it's better to have thick steaks because you cannot really sear thin ones without overcooking the middle. If the fish was large – and the best yellow-fin tuna can be enormous – one thick steak will easily feed two.

1. Bring a small saucepan of water to a simmer and add the green beans. Cook for 3–4 minutes, until they have just softened but still have a lovely crunch. Add the edamame beans and, just a minute later, drain. Briefly run the beans under cold water to prevent any further cooking and transfer to a large bowl. Peel, halve and stone the avocado and slice the flesh into wedges, roughly 1–2cm (½ in) wide. Rinse them under the cold tap to prevent browning, then add to the beans.

2. Heat the vegetable oil in a small, deep saucepan or a wok over a high heat. The oil should reach at least a third of the way up the pan. In order to test if the oil has reached temperature, drop a single noodle in the pan. If it immediately puffs up and turns white, the oil is ready. Working quickly, before the oil becomes too hot, fry the noodles in small batches. Drain the puffed noodles on kitchen paper and allow them to cool.

3. Coat the tuna steaks in olive oil and grind black pepper all over them. Heat a non-stick frying pan to very hot and sear the tuna for less than a minute on each side – it needs to be raw in the middle. Immediately the steaks are browned, transfer to a board to cool (leaving them in a pan, even off the heat, will cook the tuna through to an unappetizing grey).

4. For the dressing, put all the ingredients in a screw-top jar. Shake well.

5. Using your fingers to avoid breaking the avocado, gently toss the dressing through the greens. Serve the salad on plates, topped with a charred tuna steak and a bundle of fried vermicelli, with pickled ginger on the side. Season lightly with salt.

Chicken livers, shallots, brandy and cream on toast

Serves 2

a knob of butter

2 large banana shallots, each cut lengthways into 6 wedges

75g smoked bacon lardons

2 garlic cloves, sliced

a sprig of rosemary, leaves picked and finely chopped

2 thick slices of granary bread

butter for spreading

250g chicken livers

2 tbsp brandy

80ml single cream

1 tsp Dijon mustard

sea salt and black pepper to season

a few sprigs of watercress to serve

My local pub makes something very like this. It varies a bit: sometimes there's a slice of ham or fried mushrooms instead of the lardons. What never changes is the chicken liver, the cream and the brandy.

1. Heat half the butter in a large frying pan, over a medium-low heat, until just foaming. Add the shallots and lardons and fry, stirring frequently, until they have softened and browned, about 8 minutes. Add the garlic and rosemary and continue to cook for a further couple of minutes.

2. Take the pan off the heat, transfer the contents to a bowl and set aside. Don't wash the pan.

3. Toast the bread and lightly spread with butter. Keep warm on two serving plates.

4. To make frying the livers easier, pat them dry with kitchen paper.

5. Add the remaining butter to the frying pan and set over a high heat. When the butter is foaming, add the chicken livers and season generously with salt and pepper. Fry as fast as you dare, for 3–4 minutes, turning once or twice to brown the outside but leave the middle pink. Pour over the brandy and allow the alcohol to evaporate in all its steam and fury – chefs would set it alight at this stage to get rid of the alcohol faster, but it's not necessary. Reduce the heat to medium and return the shallots and bacon to the pan, along with the cream, mustard and a dash of hot water. Stir fast to combine, then immediately spoon onto the toast.

6. Serve with fresh green watercress, sea salt and the black pepper mill.

The trick with this simple dish is to work fast: it's easy to overcook the livers. I assemble all the ingredients so that I have them to hand as I need them, especially for Step 5, when almost all the ingredients go into the pan in a matter of minutes.

Red pepper
and broad bean salad

Serves 6

4 red peppers

1 red onion

4 tbsp olive oil

3 garlic cloves, sliced

350g frozen broad beans

150g beansprouts

3 tbsp mint leaves, roughly chopped

a small handful of pecans, roughly chopped

salt and pepper to season

crusty warm bread to serve

For the basil oil

2 handfuls of basil leaves

1 garlic clove, sliced

about 75ml olive oil

a good pinch of sea salt

1 tsp runny honey

juice of ½ lemon

I used to peel the outer skin of the peppers with a potato peeler because somewhere I'd picked up the idea that the skin was indigestible. I've since decided there's no need: fresh tender peppers are easy to find and it's a waste of good flavour and a waste of time. Use only red or yellow peppers for this, as they are much sweeter than green ones.

1. Heat the oven to 180°C/fan 160°C/gas mark 4.

2. Cut the peppers into quarters, remove the seeds and stalks and lay the pieces in a roasting tin. Peel the onion and cut, from bulb end to tip, into roughly eight wedges. Add these to the tin, then drizzle over the olive oil and scatter with the garlic. Season, and roast in the oven for 45 minutes. The pepper flesh will collapse and its sweetness will intensify.

3. Meanwhile, bring a medium saucepan of salted water to the boil. Add the broad beans and cook for just 3 minutes. Drain and rinse under cold water to halt the cooking. Squeeze each one gently to pop it from its tough outer skin.

4. Make the basil oil by putting two-thirds of the basil leaves in a blender with the garlic, a generous glug of the oil, the salt and the honey. Blitz to make a rough purée, adding more oil if it seems too thick. Stir in the lemon juice, taste, and adjust the seasoning.

5. Using your hands, combine the broad beans, beansprouts, mint and the remaining basil in a large mixing bowl. Add the warm peppers and half the basil oil and mix gently. Tip the salad onto a serving dish and pour the rest of the basil oil into a bowl or jug.

6. Heat the pecans, briefly, in a dry frying pan until just toasted. Cool a little and scatter over the salad.

7. Serve with warm bread and the extra basil oil.

Popping the emerald-green broad beans from their wrinkly skins takes a while but is well worth it. Frozen broad beans hardly need any cooking at all.

Bone-marrow baked potatoes with avocado

Serves 2

1 large baking potato

2 beef marrow bones

1 ripe avocado

salt and pepper to season

I dare say some readers might shudder at the thought of bone marrow: either because it's so gloopy or because it's so fattening, or just because it's 'offal'. Well, please, please, if that's you, just give it a try. The bone marrow melts like butter (and who doesn't like butter on a baked potato?) and the avocado turns it into a feast of rich, fresh deliciousness, a huge cut above the pedestrian baked potato with cheese. Sometimes you can get free marrow bones from the butcher because few people buy them any more. But even if I had to pay the price of fillet steak for them, I'd think them worth it. My dad used to eat bone marrow on toast; the French (and classically trained chefs) still love it melting on top of a steak; and increasingly, smart gastropubs are serving it in all sorts of imaginative ways. But for me, this is the way to eat it.

1. Heat the oven to 200°C/fan 180°C/gas mark 6.

2. Prick the potato, once on each side, with a fork. Bake the potato and marrow bones on a baking tray on the centre shelf of the oven for 1 hour and 20 minutes or until the potato skin is crisp and the centre is soft. Test with a skewer to make sure.

3. Meanwhile, halve the avocado, remove the stone, scoop out the flesh and cut it into cubes. Put these into a colander or sieve and rinse under a cold tap. This keeps the avocado from going brown, I promise.

4. When the potato is done, remove it and the marrow bones from the oven. Carefully cut the potato in half and, without damaging the skin, scoop the flesh into a bowl and chop it roughly. Scrape out the marrow from the bones with a marrow scoop or the handle of a teaspoon and add it to the potato. Add most of the avocado, then season with salt and pepper.

5. Mix gently, spoon back into the potato skins, top with the remaining avocado and serve. Nothing like it!

Sweetcorn works instead of the avocado. And if you really can't face marrow, then avo and sweetcorn together, with lots of butter, is good.

Warm potato salad
with pickled red onion

Serves 6 generously

1.2kg Désirée potatoes,
skin left on

5 spring onions, finely
sliced on the diagonal

a small handful of dill,
chopped

2 tsp capers, rinsed under
cold water

For the pickle

1 large red onion,
very thinly sliced

100ml white wine vinegar

½ tsp caster sugar

5 twists of the black
pepper mill

6 coriander seeds

For the dressing

4 tbsp olive oil

juice of ½ lemon

1 tsp Dijon mustard

salt and pepper to season

I've always thought of what are now fashionably called 'crushed' potatoes as 'Irish' potatoes. In French *haute cuisine*, you only get *pommes mousseline* (very creamy mash), whole or neatly shaped potatoes. But many spuds refuse to conform, falling apart before they are quite cooked. My favourite variety of potatoes for this dish is Désirée, which are quite well behaved and need a little bashing to fall apart, but have irresistible pink skins which look good and taste particularly earthy.

1. Combine the pickle ingredients in a glass or ceramic bowl with 200ml water and leave to marinate for at least 45 minutes. Overnight will give a stronger flavour.

2. Cut the potatoes in half (or quarter if very large) and bring to the boil in a medium-sized saucepan of salted water. Simmer for about 15–18 minutes, until the potatoes are tender.

3. Meanwhile, make the dressing by combining the olive oil, lemon juice and mustard in a screw-top jar. Add salt and pepper and shake well.

4. When the potatoes are cooked, drain and tip into a large bowl. Immediately crush them slightly or break them up with a knife to allow the steam to escape and the potatoes to dry out a bit. Then, while they are still very hot, pour over the dressing. Gently mix half the spring onions, dill and capers into the potatoes, trying not to mash the potatoes much.

5. Just before serving, drain the pickle. Transfer the potatoes to a serving dish and sprinkle with the pickled onion and the remaining greenery and capers. Serve warm or cold.

Roasted parsnips and orzo with dukkah

Serves 6

3 parsnips, scrubbed clean

3 carrots, scrubbed clean

2–3 tbsp sunflower oil

2 tbsp dukkah plus extra to serve

a pinch of salt

200g orzo

a few drops of olive oil

For the dressing

2 tbsp olive oil

1 tbsp runny honey

juice of 1 lemon

1 garlic clove, crushed

salt and pepper to season

To serve

a small handful of parsley leaves, roughly chopped

40g hazelnuts, roughly chopped

The thing that makes this combination unusual is the dukkah, a dried herb and spice mix widely available in supermarkets. Dukkahs vary, but most contain hazelnuts (so if cooking for an allergy sufferer, check the ingredients carefully), cumin, coriander and sesame. I add fresh thyme and mint if I have any.

1. Heat the oven to 200°C/fan 180°C/gas mark 6.

2. Cut the parsnips and carrots in half lengthways and then cut each half into three. Place in a roasting tin and sprinkle over the sunflower oil, dukkah and salt. Roast for 25 minutes, turning halfway through.

3. Bring a large saucepan of water to the boil and drop in the orzo. Stir vigorously at once, to prevent the pasta sticking, and then stir occasionally during cooking. Simmer for 8 minutes and drain well, rinsing the orzo under warm water to remove any remaining starch. Tip into a large bowl and toss with a few drops of olive oil to prevent the grains sticking together.

4. Put all the dressing ingredients into a screw-top jar and shake well. Combine the roasted vegetables with the orzo. Tip in the dressing, along with most of the parsley, and mix well. Season generously. Transfer to a serving dish and sprinkle over the remaining parsley and the hazelnuts. Finish with a scattering of extra dukkah.

> If you need nut-free dukkah and can't find it, make your own by mixing together the spices and dried herbs. Cumin, coriander and thyme are essential, but otherwise anything goes!

Clockwork plate

I've spent a lot of my life bemoaning the national habit of eating take-aways while watching telly. I've bossily advocated knees-under-the-table, home-cooked meals as an essential part of family life. But, let's face it, preaching is one thing, practising is another, and our guilty pleasure is this Clockwork Plate. You eat it clockwise round the plate, starting at the top with the palest or most delicate flavours and working round to the most robust, and ending up with something sweet. It's hardly gastronomy, but getting all the leftovers out of the fridge on a Sunday evening after a busy weekend of friends and family is curiously satisfying. I decide what goes with what, then put together a picnic supper for John and me to eat while watching some Sunday-night long-frock saga. Heaven. Here is an example, but leftover recipes depend on what's in your fridge – and, sadly, I have no idea what's in yours.

Use big plates (I use pizza plates). Place half a small avocado in the middle of the plate with balsamic vinegar in its central cavity: then, starting from the top, add canapé-sized bites such as smoked salmon and cream cheese on a cracker, Gem lettuce leaf filled with salami, a couple of radishes, tapenade on a toast finger, Cheddar and sun-dried tomato on a cracker, half a small tomato with salad cream on top, olives and goat's cheese on a cracker, crudités, and ending with a few chunks of fruit and chocolate! You will need to provide cocktail sticks for things too slippery to pick up in your fingers, and a teaspoon for the avocado.

Matzo lunch for children

When my children were small, they, like every child I've ever met, preferred sweet to healthy. So I devised this open sandwich, which they had to eat from left to right: starting with the savoury and ending with the sweet. No cheating. They loved it.

Arrange stripes of ham, cucumber, sausage, tomato, Cheddar, cream cheese, pecans and strawberry jam on matzo crackers.

Meat Free

Fresh gnocchi with tomatoes and summer herbs

Serves 4

1kg ripe, plum tomatoes

about 3 tbsp olive oil

1 tsp fennel seeds

1 large onion, diced

2 large garlic cloves, sliced

150ml full-fat crème fraiche (half-fat will split during cooking)

a large handful of summer herbs, roughly chopped (dill, basil and parsley)

salt and pepper to season

grating of Parmesan or vegetarian hard cheese to serve

Potato gnocchi

500g potatoes, peeled

250g plain flour

1 medium egg, beaten

salt

Potato gnocchi are easy to make, but you can buy good fresh gnocchi (potato or pasta) in large supermarkets. You will need 500g. This dish is good baked with a sprinkling of Parmesan on top too, but I like it as here, with the herbs almost raw and brilliant green with the bright red blobs of roasted tomato.

1. Heat the oven to 180°C/fan 160°C/gas mark 4.

2. Halve the tomatoes lengthways and put them, cut-side down, in an oiled roasting tin. Sprinkle with most of the oil and the fennel seeds and season with salt and pepper. Roast for 1 hour, turning the tomatoes over halfway through cooking. When cool enough to handle, cut each tomato into smallish pieces with scissors.

3. Meanwhile, in a large frying pan, fry the onion gently in 1 tablespoon oil for 4–5 minutes until soft. Add the garlic and fry for a further minute, then set aside.

4. For the gnocchi, boil the potatoes in salted, simmering water for 20 minutes or until tender. Drain, mash, taste and season well. Mix in almost all the flour and the egg. Flour your hands and knead into a ball. Using more flour to prevent sticking, roll out into long batons 2cm (¾ in) thick. Cut these into 2cm (¾ in) pieces. See the Tip below if you want to give them a traditional gnocchi shape.

5. Cook the gnocchi for exactly 3 minutes in boiling water, then drain and spread out on a clean tea towel, separating them to prevent sticking.

6. Now back to the sauce: tip the tomatoes and their juices into the onion pan and add the crème fraiche and herbs. Very gently, combine until everything is evenly distributed. Check the seasoning, then stir the gnocchi into the sauce and serve with the Parmesan.

> To get the traditional gnocchi shape, put a table fork, preferably one with four tines, face down on a board so the tips of the tines touch the board. Shape each piece of dough into a ball and roll it gently down the tines of the fork to make grooves in its surface. You should end up with a rugby-ball shape with indentations running around it.

Spiced-up fried potato cakes with poached eggs

600g small floury potatoes, skin left on

a glug of olive oil

2 shallots or ½ small onion, finely chopped

1 garlic clove, crushed

75g Savoy cabbage, shredded

½ tsp ground turmeric

½ tsp chilli powder

a small handful of coriander leaves, chopped, plus extra to serve

juice of ½ lemon

3 tbsp gram flour plus extra to coat

3–4 tbsp vegetable oil

4 large eggs

salt and pepper

(Pictured overleaf.)

It's interesting that all over Britain we have recipes for making leftover boiled spuds delicious. I just love all those homely regional names: bubble and squeak, colcannon, rumbledethumps. These are usually made with leftover potatoes and cabbage or any other green veg that's to hand, and may or may not be formed into cakes – sometimes just a delicious fry-up. Some contain a bit of fried bacon or a grating of cheese. And if you have leftover cooked fish or chicken, why not add that too? This one is veggie and gluten-free and perfect for brunch.

1. Cook the potatoes whole, in plenty of lightly salted water. Once simmering, cook for 15 minutes or until soft. Remove from the heat and drain. Allow to steam dry for at least 10 minutes before peeling off the skins. Lightly crush the potatoes with a masher and set aside.

2. Heat the olive oil in a shallow pan and add the shallot or onion. Brown lightly, over a medium-low heat, before adding the garlic and cabbage. Fry until the cabbage is soft, about 5–6 minutes. Stir through the turmeric and chilli and cook for a further 3 minutes.

3. Add the cabbage mixture, coriander and lemon juice to the potatoes. Sift over the gram flour, then mix everything together, trying not to mash the potatoes too much.

4. Using your hands, form the mixture into four round, straight-sided large cakes. Chill for at least half an hour. Gently roll the potato cakes in a little more gram flour, coating both sides lightly and using a dry brush to remove any excess.

5. Heat the vegetable oil in a large non-stick frying pan, and when hot fry the potato cakes for 5–6 minutes until a golden brown crust has formed on the base. (If all four won't fit in the pan with enough room for you to comfortably turn them over, cook them two at a time and keep the first two warm while you do the second pair.) Carefully turn the cakes over, using a palette knife or a fish slice, and continue cooking for another 5–6 minutes to brown the second side.

6. Poach the eggs. Bring a large pan of water to the simmer. Make a whirlpool in the centre by stirring rapidly with the handle of a wooden spoon. Allow the whirlpool to almost completely subside and then crack the eggs directly into it. Poach for 3 minutes on a gentle heat. Lift the eggs out with a slotted spoon, briefly holding them over a folded tea towel to dry them a bit.

7. Serve each potato cake topped with a poached egg. Garnish with chopped coriander and a good grating of black pepper.

Because this is a gluten-free recipe I've used gram flour (derived from chickpeas) where you might expect plain flour. Happily, gram flour is great. It is often used in Indian cookery to coat vegetables and deep-fried foods. It has great thickening qualities, soaking up moisture and producing a crisp crust.

Slightly spicy minestrone soup with parsley and kale

Serves 6

100g dried haricot beans, soaked overnight to soften

1 bouquet garni (see Tip)

3 tbsp extra virgin olive oil plus extra for drizzling

1 onion, roughly chopped

2 carrots, peeled and roughly chopped

2 celery sticks, roughly chopped

½ medium red chilli, deseeded and chopped

3 garlic cloves, crushed

1 potato, peeled and roughly chopped

1 x 400g tin chopped tomatoes

2 tbsp tomato purée

1 litre good-quality stock

75g small pasta shapes

100g kale, roughly chopped

2 tbsp parsley leaves, roughly chopped

finely grated zest of 1 lemon

salt and pepper to season

grated Parmesan or vegetarian hard cheese

Traditional Italian minestrone requires everything to be chopped very finely to make a soup that's eaten as a starter. I've just adapted it to make a hearty, chunky main course.

1. Rinse the soaked beans and put into a large, heavy-based saucepan. Add the bouquet garni. Cover with roughly twice the volume of water to beans and bring to the boil. Turn down and simmer, uncovered, until the beans are soft and tender – about 1½–2 hours. Drain and set aside the softened beans, discarding the aromatics.

2. Rinse out the pan, add the olive oil and set over a low heat. Add the onion, carrots, celery, chilli, garlic and potato and 'sweat' gently, covered, for 15–20 minutes until everything is soft and the onion and celery are translucent. Stir regularly to prevent the vegetables catching.

3. Tip in the tomatoes, tomato purée and stock and bring to the boil. Turn the heat down to a simmer and cook for 20 minutes with the lid off, stirring frequently. Stir the pasta and haricot beans into the soup, cooking for a further 8–10 minutes, until the pasta is al dente.

4. Just before serving, add the kale and simmer for 4–5 minutes. If the soup is too thick, add a little more stock or water. Add the parsley and lemon zest, then season to taste. Hand round the Parmesan at the table.

This is a brilliant main course veggie supper dish, but it's also the ideal soup to make if you have stock left over from boiling a piece of ham. Watch out when seasoning as ham stock will be salty already. Dilute if necessary.

Make a bouquet garni by using string to tie together 3 stalks of fresh basil or thyme, 3 parsley stalks and a bay leaf.

If time doesn't allow for overnight soaking and lengthy cooking, substitute the dried beans with a 400g tin of cooked ones.

Homity pie with sour-cream pastry and cavolo nero

Serves 6

For the sour-cream pastry

175g plain flour

a tiny pinch of salt

150g butter, diced

90ml soured cream

1 medium egg, beaten

For the filling

350g floury potatoes, peeled and sliced

150g cavolo nero, roughly chopped

3 tbsp olive oil

1 onion, finely chopped

400g leeks (roughly 2 large), finely chopped

2 garlic cloves, finely chopped

a pinch of mustard powder

125ml double cream

a small handful of parsley leaves, chopped

100g mature Cheddar cheese, finely grated

salt and pepper to season

Basically a potato and cheese pie, this is very rich, but it makes the perfect lunch after a morning hike or doing something really energetic. Or when badly in need of comfort food and you don't mind the calories.

1. For the pastry, put the flour, salt and butter in a food processor and pulse until the butter is fully incorporated through the flour. Alternatively, put in a large bowl and rub the butter into the flour using your fingertips. Then add the soured cream and pulse for 2–3 seconds, or stir by hand until just mixed. On a lightly floured surface, roll out the pastry to form a round big enough to line the base and sides of a 26cm (10in) flan dish or loose-bottomed cake tin. Carefully lower in the pastry to form the pie base. Crimp the edges of the pastry, brush with some of the beaten egg and chill in the fridge for 30 minutes.

2. Heat the oven to 180°C/fan 160°C/gas mark 4.

3. Meanwhile, put the potatoes in a large saucepan and cover with water. Bring to the boil and simmer for 8 minutes. Add the cavolo nero to the pan and cook for a further 5 minutes. Drain once both potatoes and cavolo nero are perfectly tender. Allow them to steam dry in the colander.

4. Heat the olive oil in a large, heavy-based frying pan over a medium heat and add the onion and leeks. Sauté until really soft. Add the garlic and mustard powder and continue to cook for a minute or two. Remove from the heat and add the potatoes and cavolo nero to the pan. Stir in the cream, parsley and half of the cheese, then allow the mixture to cool slightly. Season to taste.

5. Remove the pastry case from the fridge, line loosely with a sheet of baking parchment and fill with baking beans or rice, pushing them to the edges. Bake 'blind' (i.e. without the filling) for 20 minutes, until the edges begin to colour. Remove the baking paper and beans then put the pie case back in the oven for 15–20 minutes, until golden and crisp all over. Brush the inside of the pastry case with the remaining beaten egg.

6. Spoon the potato mix into the pastry case. Sprinkle with the remaining cheese and bake for 25–30 minutes. If using a loose-bottomed tin, cool for 10 minutes then lift out. Serve in slices – hot, warm or completely cold. All are delicious.

Mash hash

(All pictured overleaf.)

Carrots with ginger, parsnips with honey, and peas with mint are all familiar flavours. But puréed and served together with toast they make a healthy, pretty and unusual lunch or supper; they're also great dips to go with drinks. If you make all three purées, you should end up with enough for twenty-five people for dips with drinks, or it could be supper for six or eight, depending on the bread or toast you serve alongside. I serve these with toasted focaccia or sourdough and spread them rather greedily.

Carrot and ginger

300g young carrots, scrubbed clean

4cm (1½ in) piece of ginger, peeled

about 30g butter

a dash of olive oil plus extra for drizzling

salt and pepper to season

a small handful of sunflower seeds to serve

1. Bring a little water (a depth of roughly 4cm/1½ in) to the boil in a saucepan into which a steamer basket fits.

2. Cut the carrots in half widthways. Put the carrots in the steamer basket and set over the simmering water. Cover and steam until tender, roughly 10 minutes.

3. Empty the carrots into a food processor. Finely grate the ginger and add that to the carrots, along with the butter and olive oil. Pulse until completely smooth. Season to taste and add a little more butter if a softer consistency is required.

4. Decant into a bowl and top with a drizzle of olive oil, freshly ground pepper and a scattering of sunflower seeds. Serve warm.

Parsnip and honey

300g parsnips (about 2), scrubbed clean

1 tbsp olive oil

1 tbsp honey plus a little extra for drizzling

a pinch of ground cumin

about 100ml single cream

salt and pepper to season

1 tbsp coriander leaves, very finely chopped, to serve

1. Heat the oven to 200°C/fan 180°C/gas mark 6.

2. Cut the parsnips into even-sized chunks. Put them in a roasting tin with the olive oil, honey and cumin. Roast for 20–25 minutes until golden and beautifully caramelized.

3. Remove from the oven and allow to cool slightly. Roughly chop and then put in a food processor with the cream. Pulse until you have a smooth, soft purée, adding a touch more cream if needed. Taste and season as required.

4. Spoon into a small bowl and serve just warm, with a drizzle of honey and touch of coriander.

Pea, shallot and mint

300g frozen peas

a dash of olive oil

1 shallot or ¼ onion, finely sliced

1 garlic clove, crushed

50ml hot vegetable stock

a handful of mint leaves, chopped, plus extra to garnish

salt and pepper to season

1. Empty the peas into a large colander or sieve and pour a kettle's worth of boiling water over the top of them. Leave the steaming peas to sit for a few minutes while you move onto the shallot.

2. Heat the olive oil in a heavy-based frying pan over a medium heat. Add the shallot and gently fry until soft, but not coloured.

3. Add the garlic and cook for a further minute before adding the peas to the pan. Stir well and warm through. Pour over the hot stock, stir and remove from the heat.

4. Pulse the mixture in a food processor, or purée with a hand-held blender, adding the mint once it is smooth. Season well and spoon into a small bowl. Garnish with the extra mint leaves. Serve warm.

Squash tatin
with harissa butter

Serves 6

1 butternut squash
(about 800g), peeled
and cut into 2–3cm
(1in) rounds

1 tbsp coriander seeds

1 tbsp thyme leaves

3 tbsp olive oil

40g salted butter

1 tbsp maple syrup

1 tsp cumin seeds

2 tsp harissa paste

500g all-butter puff pastry

salt and pepper to season

a small handful of mint
leaves to serve

If you like American pumpkin pie, you'll love this. It's a savoury dish that's a bit sweet, but spicy too, and huge fun to make.

1. Heat the oven to 220°C/fan 200°C/gas mark 7. Put the squash in a large roasting tin, seeds and all. Add the coriander seeds, thyme and 2 tablespoons of the oil, then mix well. Spread out evenly and season with salt and pepper. Roast for 25 minutes, turning halfway through.

2. Meanwhile, put the remaining olive oil, along with the butter, maple syrup and cumin seeds, in a 24cm (9½ in) ovenproof frying pan over a medium heat. Heat, swirling until bubbling, for about a minute, then remove from the heat and add the harissa paste. Arrange the roasted squash slices flat on the base of the frying pan, on top of the mixture. Use all the slices, adding a second layer if needed. Allow to cool slightly.

3. On a lightly floured surface, roll out the pastry until it is about 4mm (¼ in) thick and large enough to cover the frying pan. Using the rolling pin to pick the pastry up, carefully drape it over the squash, letting the edges overhang the sides of the pan. Trim off the excess pastry with scissors, leaving about 1cm (½ in) all the way round, to allow for 'shrinking' as it cooks. Tuck the overhanging pastry down between the squash and the frying pan. Make a few slits in the pastry to allow the steam to escape.

4. Bake for 30 minutes, until brown. Leave to cool for 10 minutes. Place a lipped serving plate upside down over the pastry, then, using oven gloves, carefully flip the whole thing over. Remove the pan, replacing any escaped slices of squash, if needed. Scatter with the mint and serve.

If you want to use ready-rolled puff pastry, you will need two boxes for this. It needs to be a little colder than room temperature when you roll it, but not too rigid. Place one sheet on top of the other, then roll out.

If the butternut squash is too juicy it may not caramelize. You could cheat by heating 1 tablespoon of sugar with a splash of lemon juice or vinegar, swirling over a high heat, until you have a bubbling caramel, which you can then pour over the finished tart.

Green spinach, sprouts and frozen peas

Serves 8

2 garlic cloves, crushed

30g butter

500g Brussels sprouts, tough outer leaves peeled off

180g baby spinach leaves

a handful of wild garlic leaves, plus a few extra to garnish (optional)

250g frozen peas

300ml double cream

¼ tsp freshly grated nutmeg

salt and pepper to season

Sprouts get a bad press because they used to be big and bitter. Now they are young and sweet and cook in minutes. If serving them whole, don't bother to make that cross in the bottom unless they are very large. Peel off any very dark outer leaves.

Here is my favourite recipe for sprouts, guaranteed to win over all sprout haters. I always serve it with the Christmas turkey, and at other times of the year whenever I need green veg for a dinner party. Sometimes, usually as leftovers, it ends up with a poached egg on top for supper.

The thing is, you can prepare this in advance and reheat in the microwave, or in a wok or big saucepan, without danger of the greens losing their colour. Last time I made this, I had nothing but frozen veg to hand and it worked a treat.

1. In your smallest saucepan, fry the garlic gently in the butter until foaming and smelling good, but don't let it get brown. Remove from the heat but leave in the pan.

2. Boil the sprouts in plenty of salted water until just tender (about 5 minutes), then drain and swish them under the cold tap briefly to halt the cooking. While they are still pretty hot, decant into a food processor and pulse until roughly chopped (this step can, of course, be done by hand – it will just take longer). Spread out the chopped sprouts on a clean tea towel to steam dry a bit more.

3. In the pan you used for the sprouts, cook the spinach leaves and wild garlic, if using, in a teacup of water over a medium-low heat, turning them until they are all wilted. Drain and rinse under cold water, then dry and chop roughly. Now put the peas into the saucepan, pour boiling water over them, wait a minute for them to thaw, then drain.

4. Pour the cream into the garlic pan. Add the nutmeg, a good few twists of the pepper mill and a generous pinch of salt. Mix the three veg together and put them into a microwaveable serving dish. Pour the garlicky cream over the top and fork the top a bit to encourage the pepper and nutmeg to penetrate. Cover and refrigerate if not serving right away.

5. When ready to eat, microwave for 3 minutes, forking them over halfway through. Serve with a few wild garlic leaves, if using.

Summer veg crumble

150g butter, chilled and diced

300g plain flour

4 tarragon stalks, leaves picked and finely chopped

1 tsp mustard powder

80g Cheddar cheese, grated

For the filling

50g butter

2 garlic cloves, finely sliced

1 leek, trimmed and sliced into thin rounds

200g runner beans, sliced on the diagonal into 3cm (1in) pieces

300g asparagus, sliced into 3cm (1in) lengths

200g green beans, trimmed and cut into bite-sized pieces

salt and pepper to season

This is a good quick recipe for a vegetarian lunch. I make it with any fresh green veg – little florets of broccoli and cauliflower with a scattering of caraway seeds work well. Or you can vary the crumble by adding nuts to it or swapping the Cheddar for a blue cheese.

1. Heat the oven to 180°C/fan 160°C/gas mark 4. Grease a baking tray.

2. To make the crumble, rub the butter into the flour until the mixture resembles coarse breadcrumbs. Add half the tarragon (reserving the rest for the filling), the mustard powder and the cheese. Mix thoroughly, creating small clusters of crumble mix.

3. Liberally sprinkle the crumble mix onto the baking tray and bake in the oven for 20–25 minutes, stirring carefully halfway through cooking. Bake until very slightly browned.

4. For the filling, melt the butter in a large saucepan or wok and fry the garlic for a minute – just until you can smell the aroma but the garlic has not yet browned.

5. Add all the veg, the remaining tarragon and a coffee cup of water. Stir-fry over a medium-high heat for about 10 minutes, until the veg are all just cooked and the liquid has evaporated. You may need to add a splash more water if the veg are in danger of catching before they are cooked. Season with salt and pepper.

6. Tip into a serving dish or onto individual plates and top with the crumble mix. Serve.

The crumble topping freezes well, either raw or baked. I often make too much and keep a bag of it in the freezer. I do the same for sweet crumbles, which makes labelling them correctly rather vital!

Multi-grain risotto with blistered padron peppers

Serves 4

2 tbsp olive oil

a knob of butter

1 onion, finely chopped

2 garlic cloves, finely chopped

150g Arborio rice

100g pearled barley

100g pearled spelt

1 litre hot vegetable stock

300g padron peppers, stalks removed

50g Parmesan or vegetarian hard cheese, grated, plus extra to serve

salt and pepper to season

For the herb butter

75g soft butter

25g bunch of dill, stalks removed

25g bunch of chives

I'd never cooked with spelt until a few years ago when all sorts of wonderful whole grains – ancient wheats like farro (also called emmer) and spelt, and other grains like buckwheat and quinoa – became available, at first in health food shops and then in supermarkets. More traditional carbs that had fallen out of fashion, like barley, black rice and wild rice, were now back on the shelves. Nearly all of them, and the grain-like pasta orzo, make great risotto-style supper dishes or side dishes to go with meat. Worth a try.

If you don't already know them, my advice would be to buy a packet, and follow one of the recipes on the back. Or have a go at this one: the mixed grains give the risotto an interesting texture and nutty flavour.

1. Heat half the olive oil and the butter in a large, fairly deep, frying pan. Add the onion and garlic and sauté over a low heat until translucent and very soft. Stir in the rice, barley and spelt until all coated in the buttery oil. Begin to add the hot stock, a ladleful at a time, letting each ladleful be absorbed before adding the next. Keep adding the stock, stirring constantly, for 20–25 minutes, until all of the liquid has been absorbed and all the grains are soft and plump but still separate.

2. For the herb butter, combine the ingredients in a food processor, and pulse until smooth.

3. Put the padron peppers in a frying pan with the remaining tablespoon of olive oil over a high heat. Fry for 3 minutes, shaking the pan every so often, until the peppers are blistered and softened.

4. Stir the blistered peppers and the Parmesan through the risotto. Season to taste with freshly ground black pepper (be wary of extra salt, the stock may contain enough). Serve in warm bowls with an extra grating of Parmesan and the herb butter.

> If you can't find padron peppers then any green pepper will do. Just remove the stalk, seeds and pith and cut the flesh into big chunks. It will be slightly more muted in flavour, but delicious.

Ratatouille: the luscious one

(Pictured overleaf.)

Rat-a-tat (as it's known in my house) can be luscious, heavy on the olive oil and cooked to a rich stew. My local fishmonger, a Frenchman, makes it like that and I can't resist buying a carton every time I go in there. This version keeps for 4–5 days in the fridge and freezes well.

Serves 4

5 tbsp extra virgin olive oil

1 aubergine, cut into 1.5cm (¾ in) cubes, skin and all

1 large red pepper, cored, deseeded and sliced into strips

2 red onions, finely sliced

3 sprigs of thyme, leaves picked

1 garlic clove, finely sliced

1 courgette, green or yellow, cut into 1.5cm (¾ in) cubes

5 ripe tomatoes, roughly chopped

1 tbsp balsamic vinegar

a pinch of caster sugar

a pinch of ground coriander

salt and pepper to season

To serve

a handful of basil leaves

finely grated zest of ½ lemon

1. Heat half the oil in a large, heavy-based saucepan over a fairly high heat. Add the aubergine and fry fast, tossing the cubes until they're slightly soft and golden. Tip out into a bowl and add another glug of oil to the pan. Add the pepper and onions and fry over a medium-high heat until slightly charred and softened, about 10 minutes.

2. Lower the heat and add the rest of the olive oil, along with the thyme, garlic, courgette and tomatoes. Cook for a few minutes before adding the balsamic vinegar, sugar and coriander.

3. Simmer the ratatouille gently, stirring occasionally (or cook it, covered, in an ovenproof casserole in a medium-hot oven) for about 1 hour until the vegetables have become tender, brown and stew-like. Taste and season well with salt and pepper. Add the basil and lemon zest at the last-minute to give it a fresh kick.

Ratatouille:
the vibrant one

(Pictured overleaf.)

This version is light, fresh, and colourful; wonderfully scented with olive oil, garlic and basil, it's perfect for eating on the day of cooking. It will lose its freshness after a couple of days in the fridge, though, and comes out of the freezer watery.

1. Proceed exactly as opposite, but stop at the end of Step 2, when the veg are still bright in colour and the courgettes are just cooked.

2. Garnish with the basil and lemon zest and serve.

If you are making massive quantities of the luscious ratatouille, try this catering trick to speed up the frying. In very hot olive oil (not the expensive extra virgin) briefly deep-fry all the vegetables separately, except for the tomatoes. Stand back as you carefully lower the deep-frying basket of veg into the oil – they will splutter a bit, especially the courgettes. Once they are softened and beginning to brown, drain them well on kitchen paper, then tip into the saucepan with the tomatoes and flavourings and proceed from Step 2.

Hot rat-a-tat is great with lamb. Or on toast topped with pitted black olives.

White bean stew with porcini

Serves 8

400g dried haricot beans, soaked in water for at least 5 hours or overnight

1 garlic bulb

40g dried porcini

2 tbsp olive oil

a knob of butter

2 small onions, sliced

2 celery sticks, finely sliced into crescents

a small handful of sage leaves, roughly chopped

3 bay leaves

To serve

75g baby spinach leaves

4–5 tbsp crème fraiche

salt and pepper to season

2 tbsp flat-leaf parsley leaves, roughly chopped

The amazingly delicious fresh porcini are only available in autumn and they are very dear, but the dried porcini I've used here are less expensive and work well.

A word of warning: the length of time it takes to cook dried pulses depends on their age; if they have been sitting in the cupboard for a long time, they really will need soaking overnight in water to soften.

1. Drain the soaked haricot beans and tip them into a large saucepan or flameproof casserole. Cut the entire bulb of garlic horizontally into two halves and nestle both halves in among the beans. Cover with cold water and bring to the boil. Reduce the heat to a simmer and cook the beans for 1–1½ hours or until tender. Top up with water if necessary. Drain the beans and transfer to a bowl. Fish out the garlic halves and pop the softened cloves from their skins into the beans.

2. Meanwhile, soak the dried porcini in 400ml boiling water for 15 minutes. Drain the mushrooms, reserving the liquid, and roughly chop.

3. Put the olive oil and butter into the rinsed-out bean pot and place on a medium heat. Add the onions and celery and fry until soft, then add the sage and continue to cook for a further minute. Stir through the porcini mushrooms, beans and garlic. Nestle in the bay leaves, then pour over the reserved porcini soaking liquid.

4. Reduce the heat to low and allow to bubble at a languorous pace for 30 minutes, until the sauce has both thickened and reduced in quantity. The beans should be really soft. Remove from the heat and stir through the spinach just before serving, allowing the leaves to wilt in the warmth of the stew. Stir through the crème fraiche and season well. Serve in bowls, garnished with freshly chopped parsley.

> Dried, so-called 'wild mushrooms' (they are unlikely to be really wild) or dark fresh field mushrooms are a good substitute for the dried porcini. If using field mushrooms or fresh porcini they won't need soaking: just slice them and fry with the onions and celery.

Mushroom moqueca

Serves 4

250g chestnut mushrooms, sliced

200g oyster mushrooms, sliced

about 3 tbsp coconut oil

4 spring onions, green and white parts kept separate, chopped

1 red pepper, cored, deseeded and thinly sliced

3 garlic cloves, finely chopped

1 small red chilli, deseeded and finely chopped

1 heaped tsp smoked paprika

4 plum tomatoes

300ml unsweetened coconut cream

1 plantain or green banana, sliced into 1cm (½ in) rounds

juice of 1 lime plus wedges to serve

a handful of coriander leaves, roughly chopped

salt and pepper to season

The traditional Brazilian moqueca stew is made with fish and is lovely. But when I made it with mushrooms instead, I thought it better. The strong flavours of the peppers, tomatoes, garlic and fried plantain rather overwhelm the seafood, but the mushrooms have the oomph to hold their own. It makes a good lunch dish, rather like a substantial soup. I like it with rice or mashed potatoes. But in Brazil it was served on its own and we ate it with a spoon.

1. Fry the mushrooms in a small splash (about 1 tablespoon) of the coconut oil in a large, heavy-based saucepan over a high heat until tender. Lift them out into a bowl, add a little more coconut oil to the pan and reduce the heat to medium. Fry the white parts of the spring onions and the red pepper until soft, then add the garlic, chilli and paprika to the pan and continue to cook for a minute or two.

2. Peel the tomatoes: using a sharp knife, cut a small slit in the skin of each tomato. Bring a pan of water to the boil, plunge in the tomatoes and leave for 15–20 seconds or until the skin starts to peel back where you made the slit. Lift them out and drop them into cold water to prevent overcooking, which would result in some of the flesh coming off as well as the skin. As soon as they are cool enough to handle, peel off the skin, cut each in half and scoop out the seeds with a teaspoon. Cut into wedges.

3. Add the tomatoes to the spring onion and peppers in the pan and cook on a gentle heat, covered, for 5 minutes or until the tomatoes are soft. Stir in the mushrooms and their juices, along with the coconut cream, gently stirring to combine.

4. Meanwhile, heat a tablespoon of coconut oil in a separate frying pan over a medium-high heat and add the plantain slices. Fry until golden (about a minute on each side).

5. Taste and season the moqueca with salt and pepper. Add the lime juice. Tip into a warm serving bowl, and sprinkle over the coriander and green parts of the spring onions. Serve with lime wedges and fried plantain.

Aubergine and squash lasagne with almonds

Serves 6

2 onions, sliced

7 tbsp olive oil plus extra for greasing

2 large garlic cloves, chopped

½ medium red chilli, deseeded and chopped

2 tsp ground coriander

4 tbsp tomato purée

3 x 400g tins chopped tomatoes

150ml hot vegetable stock

1 tsp soft brown sugar

salt and pepper to season

1 tbsp parsley, chopped

100g ground almonds

2 large aubergines (about 500g)

1 large butternut squash, peeled, halved lengthways and deseeded

4–5 sprigs of thyme, leaves picked

50g flaked almonds

a large handful of basil leaves, chopped, plus extra leaves to garnish

This recipe has everything going for it. Vegan, gluten-free, healthy, delicious, looks good, freezes well, reheats perfectly, and the almonds give a great crisp texture.

1. Cook the onions in 3 tablespoons of the oil in a saucepan over a medium heat for 8 minutes until collapsed and golden. Add the garlic, chilli and ground coriander. Cook, stirring, for a couple more minutes, then add the tomato purée, tinned tomatoes, stock and sugar. Simmer for 30–40 minutes, uncovered, or until the sauce has reduced and is lovely and thick. Stir every so often. Season to taste and add the parsley and ground almonds.

2. Heat the oven to 200°C/fan 180°C/gas mark 6.

3. Cut the aubergines and squash into long, narrow 5mm (¼ in) thick slices. Brush with the remaining oil, season and lay out on two large baking trays in single layers. Top with the thyme and roast at the top of the oven for 25 minutes, swapping the trays around halfway, until both vegetables are tender and beginning to brown.

4. Oil a 2-litre ovenproof dish (or six smaller dishes to make six mini-lasagnes). Start with the six biggest squash slices, top them with sauce, then add a layer of aubergine, more sauce and so on until you have finished the ingredients. Finish with a sauce layer. Sprinkle with the flaked almonds and chopped basil.

5. Bake for 25 minutes until a skewer will glide easily through the lasagne from top to bottom. Garnish with a sprig of basil before serving. Use a fish slice to serve.

Sweet potatoes would also work well in this recipe instead of the butternut squash.

Smoked Cheddar, chive and roast beetroot gougère

Serves 4

For the filling

300g beetroot (approximately 2), trimmed, peeled and cut into 2cm (¾ in) wedges

1 tsp ground coriander

1 tbsp vegetable oil

For the white sauce

30g butter

30g plain flour

250ml whole milk

50g smoked mature Cheddar cheese (such as Applewood), grated

a small bunch of chives, finely chopped

For the gougère

70g plain flour

¼ tsp salt

a pinch of cayenne pepper

60g unsalted butter, chopped

2 medium eggs, lightly beaten

45g smoked mature Cheddar cheese, grated

10g dried breadcrumbs

I've never been a fan of smoked cheese, but this dish has converted me. It is a simply delicious, indulgent supper dish, with the old-fashioned homely beetroot filling modernized and gingered up by the coriander and smoked cheesy flavour. It needs a green vegetable or salad with it.

1. Heat the oven to 200°C/fan 180°C/gas mark 6.

2. For the filling, put the beetroot wedges on a baking tray and sprinkle with the ground coriander. Add the oil and mix well. Transfer to the oven and roast for 35–40 minutes, turning halfway through.

3. For the white sauce, melt the butter in a medium saucepan over a medium-low heat. When foaming, add the flour and mix with a wooden spoon until smooth. Cook, stirring, for 1 minute. Add the milk a little at a time, stirring to make a smooth sauce. Bring to a simmer and cook for a minute. Remove from the heat and stir in the cheese, most of the chives and the roasted beetroot.

4. For the gougère, mix the flour with the salt and cayenne, then sift onto a sheet of baking parchment. Melt the butter in a saucepan with 150ml water, bring to the boil, then shoot in the flour all at once. Remove the pan from the heat and, with a wooden spoon, beat really vigorously for a minute, until the mixture is smooth and comes away from the sides of the pan. Set aside to cool for a few minutes.

5. Gradually beat the eggs into the cooled gougère mixture, so that it becomes smooth and shiny and rather reluctantly drops off the spoon, then stir in the cheese. Using a dessert spoon, dollop this mixture all around the edge of a 20cm (8in) round or oval shallow ovenproof dish. Spoon the filling into the middle, sprinkle over the breadcrumbs and bake for 35 minutes. Garnish with the remaining chives and serve.

> Gougère is a version of choux pastry. If you are new to making it, you need to know that speed is of the essence. Being slow in adding the flour (using a paper funnel to shoot the flour into the liquid in one go helps), any pause before beating or stirring rather than beating like blazes, will leave you with half-cooked lumps of flour.

Soft polenta with garlic field mushrooms and kale

Serves 4

a knob of unsalted butter

a glug of olive oil

3 banana shallots, peeled and quartered lengthways

4 large field mushrooms or chestnut mushrooms (about 300g), cleaned and sliced

4 garlic cloves, finely sliced

150g kale, tough stalks removed and leaves torn into bite-sized pieces

200ml hot vegetable stock

salt and pepper to season

For the polenta

1 litre vegetable stock

200g fine polenta

100ml single cream

50g butter

50g Parmesan or vegetarian hard cheese, finely grated

To serve

a small handful of pine nuts, toasted

truffle oil (optional)

I used not to be a fan of polenta, because it is so often bland and boring, or, when fried, tough, bland and boring! But I now have the zeal of the converted. I love it. You do have to season it well, and for me that usually means plenty of strong-flavoured cheese like the Parmesan here, or something with power to go with it. In this recipe the polenta is a blank canvas, so taste and season it well to make a delicious backdrop to these simple, seasonal ingredients. It is also very quick to put together.

1. Heat the butter and olive oil in a large, heavy-based frying pan or a wok over a medium-high heat and add the shallots. Sauté for 5 minutes or until they are just soft. Add the mushrooms and garlic to the pan – it will be stuffed full but keep frying and within a few minutes, the mushrooms will shrink and everything will become manageable.

2. Keeping the heat high, add the kale and stock and continue to cook until the leaves wilt and soften. Season with salt and pepper. Turn down the heat to low and keep warm while you cook the polenta.

3. For the polenta, bring the stock to the boil in a medium saucepan. Slowly pour in the polenta, stirring constantly. Simmer for 5–10 minutes (while stirring frequently and scraping the bottom to prevent scorching) until thickened and pulling away from the sides of the pan.

4. Remove from the heat and stir in the cream, butter and Parmesan. Taste and season well, then spoon onto plates. Top with the mushroom and kale mixture, and serve sprinkled with a few pine nuts and a drizzle of truffle oil, if you like.

It is worth remembering that the longer polenta stands, the firmer it becomes, so be swift to serve this dish. If it does firm up too much, add a little more stock just before plating up. The ideal consistency is similar to a soft risotto.

Feasts

Salami and pumpernickel party bites

a small handful of parsley, basil or coriander leaves, or a mixture

150g cream cheese

6 slices of pumpernickel or rye bread

about 50g soft butter

200g thinly sliced soft salami, skin removed

(Pictured overleaf.)

These snacks are really easy to do, they freeze well and are soon gobbled up by friends with a glass in the other hand. The assembly instructions below, now I re-read them, sound rather complicated, but if you just follow them step by step you will get alternating colours, like liquorice allsorts. When buying salami from a deli, ask for the skin to be removed before slicing and for the slices to be as thin as possible.

1. Chop the herbs finely, then mix them with half the cream cheese. If you have a coffee grinder or small liquidizer, a quick blitz will give you a smoother green, rather than a speckled one, but it's not vital.

2. Lay the slices of bread on a large board and spread four of them thinly with butter.

3. Now cover two of the buttered pieces with a layer of salami, piling it on until you have a good, thick, even layer. Then cover the salami with the other two pieces of buttered bread, buttered side down.

4. You will now have plain unbuttered sides of bread on top of your two stacks. Spread one thickly with the herby cheese and the other with the plain one.

5. Use the two unbuttered slices of bread to top the stacks. Press down to 'glue' the layers together, wrap with cling film or foil and refrigerate.

6. When ready to serve, use a sharp knife to neaten the edges and cut each stack into twelve neat blocks.

> If you can't get really soft salami, you could use cured chorizo: skin it and blitz to an orange paste in the food processor.

Watermelon blocks with spiced seeds

(Pictured overleaf.)

Makes 40

¼ watermelon

2 tsp za'atar

2 tbsp sunflower seeds

2 tbsp sesame seeds

½ tsp salt

freshly ground pepper

1 tbsp nigella seeds

These are great little bites for a hot day, and are easy to do. As long as the watermelon flesh is dark red, the chances are it will be sweet and flavoursome. If there isn't a cut-open half of watermelon on the stall or the shelf, ask for one to be cut in half. Greengrocers usually sell half watermelons anyway, so if you reject it they shouldn't mind.

1. Cut the watermelon flesh into bite-sized square blocks. Leave to drain on kitchen paper to dry them a bit. Don't bother to remove the pips – they are nice and crunchy.

2. Put the za'atar, sunflower seeds and sesame seeds into a dry frying pan and toast for 3–4 minutes, shaking the pan to prevent burning. Put the seeds into a pestle and mortar with the salt. Pound to a fairly fine mix, then empty into a shallow bowl. Stir in the pepper and nigella seeds.

3. Gently press the watermelon blocks into the seeds to coat them on all sides.

4. Eat with your fingers or a cocktail stick. If the latter, don't put the sticks in the blocks before serving, because after a while the juice loosens them. Hand the blocks and sticks round separately.

The watermelon blocks will sit for an hour or two but any longer and the texture becomes a little soft.

These are also really good as a light lunch or first course with feta or goat's cheese in a salad.

Homemade root-vegetable crisps with thyme and seeds

Serves 8

2 small parsnips

1 sweet potato (about 200g)

2 large beetroot

100g mixed seeds (linseed, sesame and poppy)

½ tsp salt, plus extra to season

3 tbsp olive oil

black pepper to season

(Pictured on previous page.)

These are very fashionable now, being a lot healthier than deep-fried potato crisps. They taste delicious too. The only drawback is they shrink a lot during the cooking process and you might be wise to double the quantities here. They are very moreish.

1. Heat the oven to 200°C/fan 180°C/gas mark 6. Scrub the vegetables clean but keep the skins on. Slice each of the vegetables along its length, on the diagonal, using a mandoline or vegetable slicer – keep the beetroot separate to prevent it staining everything purple.

2. Put the parsnips and sweet potato into one medium bowl and the beetroot into another, dividing the seeds, salt and oil between the two. Gently toss together with your hands. Transfer to two or three baking trays, arranging them in a shallow layer to ensure they crisp up. Bake for 15 minutes, then remove from the oven and turn over each crisp. Return to the oven for a final 20 minutes or until dry to the touch. Remove and allow to cool on the baking trays until needed.

3. Toss both varieties together, scatter with a little more salt and black pepper and serve.

These homemade crisps soften after 12 hours or so, but if you warm them up in the oven (5 minutes at 180°C/fan 160°C/gas mark 4) they will crisp up again as they cool.

Hot garlic, chilli and parsley prawns

Serves 6

180g raw king prawns, peeled but with the tails left on

a squeeze of lemon juice to finish

For the sauce

a handful of flat-leaf parsley leaves

4 garlic cloves, halved

½ small red chilli, deseeded

½ tsp salt

100ml olive oil

(Pictured on previous page.)

This is a very easy and delicious recipe for prawns or langoustine. I love them cooked like this and served for lunch with crusty bread to mop up the sauce. The sauce is also good served cold with hot barbecued prawns, langoustine or any seafood. But the recipe here assumes the prawns are for nibbling at a party and will be handed round, maybe in a frying pan, which gives the message that they are freshly cooked from raw, not just emptied out of a packet.

1. Blitz the sauce ingredients in a food processor or liquidizer to form a rough paste.

2. Put a good tablespoon of the sauce into a frying pan and set over a high heat. Add the prawns and fry for 30 seconds. Stir in the rest of the sauce, and cook for 2–3 minutes until the prawns are just pink. Decant at once (to stop them overcooking) into a second, cold, frying pan and add a squeeze of lemon juice. (Using the pan you cooked them in risks burning a guest or the prawns overcooking. Anyway, the quickest way to cool them down to eating temp, is to tip them into a cold pan or dish.)

3. Hand them round, still warm, with cocktail sticks.

Tails on or off? I like to eat the tails of prawns, crunching them up happily, but since not everyone does, it might be better, if these are to be served at a stand-up drinks party, to remove the tails when shelling the prawns and save your friends having to hunt for a way to dispose of them. But if serving at a table, I would always leave the tails on, partly because they look better and partly for people like me who like to eat them.

Filo tartlets with mushroom duxelles and quails' eggs

Makes about 24

6–8 sheets filo pastry

50g salted butter, melted

For the filling

200g chestnut mushrooms

2 tbsp olive oil

2 garlic cloves, crushed

4 tarragon stalks, leaves picked and finely chopped

12 hard-boiled quails' eggs, halved (or 24 raw quails' eggs if poaching and serving hot, see Tip opposite)

salt and pepper to season

(Pictured overleaf.)

These little tartlets are mouthwatering. They are a bit of a fiddle to do, but worth it. Make more than you think you need. I reckon drinking guests will eat an average of five of them each if this is the only snack you are offering. As a caterer I used to serve them warm, each with a whole, poached quail's egg on top. Since I do my own catering today, I make life easier for myself and serve them cold with halved hard-boiled eggs. But see the tip opposite for the warm version which, because of the runny egg yolk, is richer. Just a word of warning: make sure the tartlets are deep rather than wide (use mini-muffin moulds, rather than mini-tartlet ones) because the yolks are runny and so guests need to eat them in one mouthful. Yolk down your best vintage cocktail dress is not a good look.

1. Preheat oven to 180°C/fan 160°C/gas mark 4.

2. You will need to work quickly, as the filo pastry will become dry if exposed to the air for too long, so ensure any sheets you are not using are well wrapped. Lay out two or three sheets of pastry at a time, on top of each other. Using a sharp knife or scissors, cut the pastry into 7cm (2½ in) squares, trimming off any ragged edges. Repeat until you have seventy-two squares.

3. Keeping any pastry you are not working with covered with cling film, take one of the pastry squares and brush with the melted butter. Lay a second square on top of it, offset by roughly 30 degrees. Brush with butter before adding a third square of pastry, again offset by roughly 30 degrees and again brushing with butter. Then mould the pastry stack into one of the dips of a mini-muffin tray to form a little cup.

4. Repeat with the remaining pastry squares to make twenty-four tartlets. Bake in batches for 5–6 minutes (take care, they burn easily) until light golden and crisp, then carefully remove the tartlets to a wire rack and leave to cool.

5. For the filling, finely dice the mushrooms. Heat the olive oil in a small saucepan over a medium heat and add the mushrooms, garlic and half the tarragon. Fry for about 10–12 minutes, until the mixture is thick and dark. Season to taste, then spoon into the prepared tartlet cases. Top with half a quail's egg and a pinch of tarragon.

You can cook the filo cases a few days beforehand and keep them in an airtight container. The mushroom filling can also be made in advance, reheated and spooned into the cases to be topped with the eggs just before your guests arrive.

To serve the tarlets hot with whole quails' eggs, make the cases and the mushroom filling as above. On the day of serving, heat a frying pan of water, add a teaspoon of white vinegar or lemon juice and a good pinch of salt. Crack 8 quails' eggs into the water to poach, positioning them in a circle so you know which went in first. They will take less than a minute to cook, just enough for the whites to be firm and the yolks still soft. With a slotted spoon, lift them out in the order they went in and carefully slide them into a bowl of cold water. Repeat with the rest of the quails' eggs. When about to serve the tartlets, fill them with the mushrooms, and reheat in a gentle oven. You want them warm, not blazing hot. Meanwhile, bring a frying pan of water to the boil and then turn it off. Lift the quails' eggs from the cold water into the hot water with a slotted spoon. They will take 30 seconds to warm up. Lift them out, gently dry on a folded tea towel and then place on the warmed tartlets. Finish with a pinch of chopped tarragon.

Goat's cheese, thyme and honey on toast

Makes 12

1 French ficelle (thin
long baguette), cut into
12 rounds

1 garlic clove, halved

175g small goat's cheese log,
not too ripe, thinly sliced
into 12 rounds

3 ripe Conference pears

about 2 tbsp runny honey

a good sprig of thyme,
leaves picked

salt and pepper to season

These are simple and delicious. You need to find bread rolls or round toasts exactly the diameter of a small goat's cheese log (about 3.5cm/ 1½ in across). I have used a French 'ficelle' (like a mini-baguette) from a French bread shop, but you could, if necessary, stamp out rounds from a sliced loaf using a cookie cutter.

1. Heat the grill to high. Arrange the slices of baguette on a baking tray. Grill until just crisp and beginning to brown, then turn over and brown the other side. Remove from the grill and immediately rub each toast with a cut side of the garlic.

2. Leaving the skin on, cut the middle section of each pear (the part that is about the same circumference as the toast and the cheese) into four thin slices.

3. Top each toast first with a slice of pear and then with a round of goat's cheese. Paint each cheese slice thinly with honey. Sprinkle with the thyme leaves. Place under the grill for 1–2 minutes, until the cheese is just starting to melt. Season to taste before serving.

> If your goat's cheese is ripe and runny, don't try to grill it. Just spread it on the pear slices, put them on the mini-toasts, and finish with the honey and thyme.

Pear and beetroot soup with crispy pancetta

Serves 6

1 tbsp olive oil

2 small red onions, roughly chopped

3 garlic cloves, finely sliced

2 celery sticks, roughly chopped

a pinch of ground cinnamon

600g beetroot, peeled and cut into 1–2cm (½ in) cubes

2 ripe pears, cored and cut into 2–3cm (1in) chunks

1.2 litres hot vegetable stock

salt and pepper to season

To serve

12 thin slices of pancetta

6 slices of brioche

This is the perfect autumn warmer: fabulous colour, spicy and filling. Add a glug of brandy and tell yourself it is medicine … bound to ward off winter colds.

1. Heat the oil in a large saucepan and add the onions, garlic and celery. Cook, covered, on a lowish heat for a good 15 minutes, until the onions and celery are soft. Stir through the cinnamon.

2. Add the beetroot and pears to the saucepan and continue to cook, covered, for 10 minutes, removing the lid to stir halfway through. Pour over the stock, cover again and simmer for 40 minutes or until the beetroot is tender and cuts like butter.

3. Use a hand-held blender or food processor to purée the soup, in batches if necessary, until smooth. Return the soup to the saucepan and warm through. Season well with salt and black pepper.

4. Heat a griddle or frying pan over a high heat and grill the pancetta until crispy. Remove from the pan and quickly do the same to the brioche, which won't take a second to toast on a hot griddle.

5. Serve the soup in bowls, each garnished with two grilled strips of pancetta. Put toasted brioche on the table.

Mussel soup
with artichoke tartines

Serves 4

500g mussels

250ml cider

2 tbsp olive oil

1 onion, finely chopped

1 large leek, trimmed and finely diced

1 green pepper, cored, deseeded and finely diced

2 garlic cloves, crushed

400ml hot vegetable stock

50g baby spinach leaves, roughly chopped

125ml double cream

salt and pepper to season

For the tartines

125g artichoke hearts, chargrilled or in brine, drained

100g cream cheese

a squeeze of lemon juice

2 rectangular slices of rye bread, halved

50g Gruyère cheese, finely grated

Mussel soup is reliably delicious, but this is unusual and pretty as well. You can assemble the tartines in advance (stopping short of the final grilling) and make the soup without adding the mussels, cream and spinach. Then, when you want to eat, add these to the liquid and reheat, and put the tartines under the grill.

1. Prepare the mussels: scrub each one, removing any sand or seaweedy 'beards'. Discard any open mussels that refuse to close even when given a sharp tap. Rinse well under cold water. Put the mussels in a saucepan with a close-fitting lid. Pour over the cider and close the lid. Cook over a high heat for 3–4 minutes, shaking the pan regularly.

2. Drain, reserving the cooking liquor, and pick the mussels from their shells, leaving 16 or so in their shells because they look so pretty. Set aside.

3. Heat the olive oil in a large saucepan over a medium heat and add the onion, leek and green pepper. Cook until soft, roughly 8–10 minutes. Add the garlic and cook for a further minute before pouring over the stock and the reserved cooking liquor. Bring to a gentle simmer and take off the heat.

4. Blitz the artichokes, cream cheese and lemon juice together to give a rough, spreadable texture. Season to taste. Heat the grill to high. Lightly toast the rye bread on both sides, cool a little, then spread with the artichoke mixture. Sprinkle with the Gruyère and grill for 2–3 minutes until the cheese forms a golden crust. Remove and keep warm.

5. Just before serving the soup, add the mussels, spinach leaves and cream to the saucepan. Season well and heat gently, without boiling, then pour into four bowls, making sure that the shell-on mussels are evenly distributed. Serve with a tartine floating on top.

No cider? A splash of white wine will do instead.

Almond, cauliflower and garlic party soup

Serves 6

1 garlic bulb

2 tbsp olive oil

1 onion, finely sliced

1 small cauliflower, broken into florets

100g ground almonds

400ml almond milk

400ml good-quality strong chicken stock

1 tsp almond essence (optional)

salt and pepper to season

To serve

2 tbsp dried rose petals or 8 small fresh red ones

a small handful of coriander leaves

2 tbsp coriander seeds, toasted or dry-fried

2 tbsp pine nuts, toasted or dry-fried

1 tbsp sumac

18 small balls of watermelon scooped out with a small melon baller or teaspoon

olive oil for drizzling

This is my current favourite dinner-party soup. It's good hot, but I prefer it chilled. I make it in advance and freeze or refrigerate it in a big plastic milk carton. When thawed, I give it another blitz in the liquidizer to make sure it is velvet-smooth and return it to the carton. Just before serving, I put wide old-fashioned soup bowls round the table, pour in the soup from the carton, then go around sprinkling a bit of each garnish onto the soups.

1. Preheat the oven to 200°C/fan 180°C/gas mark 6.

2. Cut the garlic bulb in half horizontally and wrap each half in foil. Bake in the oven for 25 minutes (or place on a covered saucer and microwave until squashy – roughly 5 minutes). When the garlic is just cool enough to handle, squeeze the soft paste out of each clove.

3. Heat the olive oil in a large saucepan over a medium-high heat. Add the onion and sweat until soft but not brown. Add the cauliflower florets, ground almonds, almond milk, stock and garlic paste into the pan. Put on a lid and cook slowly until the cauliflower is soft, about 20 minutes, stirring every so often. Taste and adjust the seasoning as needed.

4. Liquidize the soup in batches to a smooth, velvety consistency. The longer you blitz, the smoother it will be. If you wish, add a few drops of almond essence for a slightly stronger almond note. Return the soup to the pan and heat gently. Serve garnished with any or all (I use all!) of the garnishes.

If serving the soup hot you won't have time to walk round the table arranging the toppings one by one. So put all the toppings except the watermelon balls and oil into a bowl. Using deep rather than wide soup bowls, put them on a tray, pour in the hot soup and add a good scattering of the topping to each, plus the watermelon balls and a drizzle of oil.

Spinach and coconut soup

Serves 6

2 tbsp olive oil

1 onion, finely chopped

3 garlic cloves, finely chopped

5cm (2in) piece of ginger, peeled and grated

1 potato, cut into 0.5–1cm (½ in) cubes

300g spinach leaves

600ml cold vegetable stock

1 x 400ml tin coconut milk

juice of ½ lemon

grated nutmeg to taste

salt and pepper to season

single cream or toasted coconut flakes to garnish

I was first served this soup by a French-speaking chef from the Caribbean island of St Vincent. It is a glorious combination of classic French soup fused with the coconut and spice so beloved of the islands.

1. Heat a large, heavy-based saucepan over a medium heat. Add the oil and once it is hot, tip in the onion. Gently fry, stirring regularly, for 5–6 minutes or until soft before adding the garlic, ginger and potato and continue to fry, covered, for a further 7–8 minutes, until the potato softens. Add the spinach; toss until just wilted, a couple of minutes max.

2. Whizz the soup thoroughly in a liquidizer, adding enough cold stock to ensure a silky smooth texture, then tip into a large jug or bowl and add the rest of the stock, the coconut milk, lemon juice and plenty of nutmeg. Taste for an even balance of coconut and nutmeg. Season with salt and pepper. Chill well. If eating the soup hot, reheat rapidly just before serving, but don't let it boil. Serve promptly to retain the colour.

3. If serving the soup chilled for a dinner party it is fun to write the guests' names (if they are short) or initials (if they aren't) in the soup by way of place names. The trick is to make sure the soup is exactly the same consistency as that of the single cream. The cream jug must have a good narrow pouring lip. Put the plate of soup, preferably a wide shallow one to give you maximum surface area, in place, and then pour the cream from the jug to write the initials or name. If you haven't done this before, have a practice on a thin layer of soup on a side plate first.

You can write your guests' names or initials when serving hot too, but it takes a while and the soup will be cooling as you write, so it's probably pressure you don't need. Instead, you could sprinkle the top of each bowl of hot soup with a few toasted coconut flakes.

Bi-colour soups:
Pea and watercress

50g butter

1 onion, finely chopped

3 garlic cloves, finely sliced

2 celery sticks, finely chopped

1 floury potato, peeled and cubed

300g watercress, destalked, washed and roughly chopped (about 250g destalked weight)

250g frozen peas

500ml hot vegetable stock

500ml whole milk

salt and pepper to season

To garnish (optional)

2 tbsp roughly chopped dill

2 tbsp chopped mint

about 150ml crème fraiche

(Pictured overleaf.)

This soup and the Spiced Roasted Parsnip Soup (opposite) are good candidates for my 'bi-colour soups'. It's just a trick, but it does look good. You make two different-coloured smooth creamy soups, like these two. To play around with the look of the soups, such as in our pictures, it's vital that the soups are super-smooth, with the texture of single cream, so liquidize them in a powerful blender. They must have flavours that will work together and be of exactly the same thickness. Forget the suggested garnishes here, you won't need them. When serving, you hold a jug of one soup in your right hand and a jug of the other in your left and pour them simultaneously into each soup bowl. You can play around with the patterns as you pour to get a yin-yang shape, or fill each side of the bowl with contrasting soups then swirl with a spoon or knife to make feathery patterns. It only takes a few seconds and looks striking.

1. Melt the butter in a deep, heavy-based saucepan over a medium-low heat. Add a splash of water and gently fry the onion, garlic, celery and potato, stirring occasionally, until the potato is soft but not brown.

2. Add the watercress, peas and stock and bring to the boil. Remove from the heat and stir in the milk. Purée the soup in a blender, adding more milk or stock if needed to achieve a pourable, not too thick, absolutely smooth soup. Return to the heat to warm through, without boiling. Add salt and pepper to taste.

3. Pour the soup into bowls, using the above bi-colour method, if desired. Otherwise, scatter over the herbs, if using, followed by a dollop of crème fraiche.

Combinations of beetroot and potato, or leek and tomato, or butternut squash and white onion all look, and taste, great too.

Bi-colour soups:
Spiced roasted parsnip

Serves 8

800g parsnips, scrubbed and cut into 3–4cm (1½ in) cubes

4 tbsp olive oil

2 onions, chopped

1 tsp ground coriander

1 tsp ground cumin

1 tsp ground turmeric

1 tsp ground ginger

1 litre hot vegetable stock

500ml whole milk

salt and pepper to season

To garnish (optional)

100g whole cooked chestnuts, roughly chopped

olive oil for frying

2 tbsp truffle oil or to taste

(Pictured overleaf.)

This is the second of my suggested soups for the bi-colour trick (see opposite) but of course it works well on its own. If you are making both soups, don't bother with the garnishes.

1. Heat the oven to 200°C/fan 180°C/gas mark 6.

2. Arrange the parsnips in a roasting tin, drizzle with half of the olive oil and turn until coated. Roast for 30 minutes until just golden, tossing the parsnips halfway through.

3. Heat the remaining olive oil in a large saucepan over a medium heat. Add the onions and fry until soft but not coloured, about 6–8 minutes. Stir through the spices and continue to fry for a further few minutes.

4. Add the roasted parsnips and the stock to the pan. Bring to the boil, cover, and then simmer for 10 minutes. Allow to cool and then use a blender or liquidizer to purée the soup to velvety smoothness. Return to the pan and stir in the milk. Gently heat through and season to taste.

5. Pour the soup into bowls, using the bi-colour method, if desired. If adding a garnish, fry the chestnuts in a little olive oil for a minute or two. Serve the roasted parsnip soup in bowls, garnished with the hot chestnuts and truffle oil.

> Don't get carried away with the truffle oil. It can be overridingly powerful in flavour.

Butterflied sardines with slow-roast tomato and strawberries

Serves 4

450g tomatoes, halved horizontally

250g baby plum or cherry tomatoes

350g strawberries, stalks removed and halved

1 garlic clove, crushed

3 tbsp olive oil plus extra for brushing

8 fresh sardines, butterflied

juice of ½ lemon

salt and pepper to season

basil leaves to serve

This is a lovely, warm summery starter or light lunch dish. I make it with mackerel fillets or with sardines – which, if you can get them, are generally cheaper. You can buy them ready prepared, opened out and backbones removed ('butterflied'). The warm strawberry/tomato salad is good with feta too, maybe as part of a buffet. The combination of the sweet tomatoes and strawberries with the salty fish is surprising and delicious.

1. Heat the oven to 170°C/fan 150°C/gas mark 5.

2. Put the tomato halves, whole baby plum or cherry tomatoes, strawberries and garlic in a roasting tin and pour over the olive oil. Season with salt and pepper and roast for 50 minutes–1 hour until collapsed. Remove from the oven and keep warm.

3. Put the grill on high. With a razor-sharp knife, make three diagonal cuts through the skin of each sardine fillet, taking care not to go deeply into the flesh. Brush with olive oil, season with salt and black pepper, and lay them, skin side up, on a piece of oiled foil on the grill pan. When the grill is hot, slide the fish under it, and grill for 3–4 minutes until the skin is beginning to brown and crisp. Squeeze over the lemon juice.

4. Serve a spoonful of warm salad with two sardines and a few basil leaves on each plate.

Fried watermelon and prosciutto with sweet balsamic

Serves 4

1 tbsp pine nuts

1 small watermelon

8 slices of prosciutto

3 tbsp olive oil

a small handful of rocket leaves

60g feta, crumbled

a handful of pomegranate seeds

balsamic glaze to serve

salt and pepper to season

I think I invented this dish when I was asked to appear on *Saturday Kitchen* and persuade viewers that watermelon was worth eating. It was delicious, so I hope I succeeded. But I'm nervous of claiming originality ever since, in the seventies, I thought I'd invented Stilton soup (I'd just been on a press trip to Denmark and eaten Samsoe soup, and had concluded it would be even better with Stilton). I served it at Leith's Restaurant and my catering company, wrote it up in my *Daily Mail* column, and pretty soon it started appearing in magazines and on the menus of other restaurants. I was pretty pleased with myself – until I opened *Cassell's Dictionary of Domestic Economy*, published in 1925, and read a recipe for Derbyshire Stilton soup, almost identical to mine: basically a celery soup with a ton of Stilton whisked into it at the end.

1. Toast the pine nuts in a dry frying pan over a medium heat until golden. Tip out onto a saucer to cool.

2. With a large sharp knife, halve the melon across the equator and carefully cut 2.5cm (1in) wide, even slices from each half. Trim the skin from the watermelon slices, then cut eight batons about 7.5cm (3in) long. (I'm afraid you won't need the rest of the melon but you could use it to make the Watermelon Blocks with Spiced Seeds on page 117.)

3. When ready to cook, but not before or the salt in the ham will draw out the water in the melon and make it slippery, wrap a slice of prosciutto around each melon piece.

4. Heat half the olive oil in a large frying pan over a high heat. Once it is hot, fast-fry the watermelon, in batches, frying the side with the ham join first, to stop it unravelling as you turn the baton to fry on all sides. You want to fry fast enough so that the prosciutto crisps up and browns but the watermelon stays raw inside. Remove from the pan and set two batons on each serving plate.

5. Scatter over the rocket, feta, toasted pine nuts and pomegranate seeds. Drip or drizzle the rest of the olive oil over the plates, and add a touch (not more than a teaspoon per plate) of balsamic glaze to each one. Season lightly with salt (remember the ham is salty) and generously with coarsely milled black pepper.

Haddock and spring onion twice-baked soufflés

(Pictured overleaf.)

Serves 8

240g smoked haddock fillet

1 small onion, halved

1 bay leaf

300ml whole milk

45g butter

40g plain flour

a pinch of mustard powder

75g Cheddar cheese

4 medium eggs, separated

salt and pepper to season

4 spring onions, finely chopped

200ml double cream

3 tbsp finely grated Parmesan cheese

I first ate a twice-baked cheese soufflé at Le Gavroche in the seventies. I couldn't believe it. It was smooth as silk, light as air, wonderful flavour; everything a soufflé should be, but somehow richer. Which is not really surprising because the technique of twice-baked soufflés is to make standard little soufflés, allow them to cool, then put them in a deep dish and drench them in double cream. As the soufflé re-bakes it absorbs the cream, which replaces the original air pockets. So it really, really has to be worth the calories, which I think it is.

This version is slightly less rich, and each soufflé is small, so, go on – risk it. You can always follow it with something fat-free and good for you.

1. Put the haddock, onion and bay leaf in a small saucepan and cover with the milk. Bring to a simmer and cook for 4 minutes. Turn off the heat and allow the fish to sit for a further 2 minutes until just cooked through. Using a slotted spoon, remove the fish and set aside. Strain the milk into a jug, discarding the onion and bay leaf.

2. Heat the oven to 180°C/fan 160°C/gas mark 4.

3. Melt the butter in a saucepan and use a little of it to brush eight ramekins or small teacups. Stir the flour and mustard powder into the remaining butter. Cook, stirring, for 45 seconds. Off the heat, gradually stir in the milk from poaching the haddock, whisking until smooth. Return to the heat and stir until the sauce boils and thickens.

4. Remove from the heat and immediately add the Cheddar, stirring until melted and smooth, then stir in the egg yolks and season to taste.

5. Flake the haddock, removing the skin and any bones. Add to the saucepan, along with half the spring onions. Whisk the egg whites until stiff but not dry and mix a spoonful into the mixture to loosen it. Fold in the remaining egg whites then spoon into the prepared ramekins until two-thirds full.

6. Place in a deep roasting tin and pour in enough boiling water to come halfway up the sides of the moulds. Bake in the oven for 15–20 minutes or until set. Remove and allow to cool. They will sink, but don't worry.

7. Before serving, turn the oven temperature up to 220°C/fan 200°C/gas mark 7. Run a knife around the soufflés to loosen them. Turn them out, upside down, into a large, ovenproof dish. Pour over the cream, making sure the tops of all the soufflés are covered. Sprinkle with the Parmesan and the remaining spring onions. Return to the oven for 12–15 minutes or until the cream is absorbed and the tops are golden.

These little soufflés are more tolerant than ones dependent on air to hold them up, so you will have time, if you like, to dish them up individually and garnish each plate with a sprig of watercress or a few rocket leaves. Their bitterness makes a good contrast to the richness of the soufflés.

Indeed they are so tolerant you can make them the day before: just get them to the stage when you have given them their first bake (Step 6), then cool them and turn them out. Cover with cling film and refrigerate. The next day, heat the oven, cover the soufflés with cream and re-bake them.

Steak tartare with pitta bread and curd cheese

Serves 4

500g beef fillet

4 tbsp curd cheese

1 tsp salted capers, well rinsed

1 tbsp flat-leaf parsley leaves, coarsely chopped

about 4 tbsp best olive oil for drizzling

sea salt to season

For the pitta bread – makes 12

10g active dried yeast

1 tsp sugar

500g strong white flour

1 tsp mustard powder

2 tsp salt

2 tbsp olive oil plus extra for greasing

(Pictured on previous page.)

I first had this at a dinner with Hugh Fearnley-Whittingstall and, as you'd expect, it was a fresh, delicious and original take on the classic steak tartare, which is rich with egg yolk, the raw meat chopped finely and seasoned strongly. Hugh's version was made with his local beef and not much else, and served with hot fresh pitta bread, giving the beef a chance to speak for itself.

The pitta bread recipe will actually make twelve pittas, far too many for four people, so put the extra into a polythene bag the minute they are cool and refrigerate or freeze them. Reheated briefly they will still be delicious, though not puffed up. Or you could make half the quantity.

1. First make the pitta dough. Put 100ml warm water in a jug and sprinkle in the yeast and the sugar. Leave for 10 minutes until small bubbles appear on the surface.

2. Mix the flour, mustard powder and salt in a large bowl. Pour over the yeast mixture, the oil and 300ml warm water (adding it a little at a time). Using your hands, mix well to create a soft, pliable dough, then transfer to a lightly floured surface and knead until soft and elastic, about 8–10 minutes. Return the dough to a clean, oiled bowl and cover with a damp tea towel or oiled cling film. Leave in a warm place for about 1½ hours or until doubled in size.

3. Divide the dough into approximately 80g balls, cover with a damp tea towel and allow to rest for 10 minutes, then roll out on a floured surface to rounds about 5mm (¼ in) thick, making sure they are of an even thickness all over. Again, cover with a damp tea towel and leave for 20 minutes.

4. Move onto the tartare. Trim the beef fillet to remove any sinew. Take the sharpest knife you own and cut the beef into thin slices, about 2.5–5mm (¼ in) thick. Cut the slices again crossways, forming very thin strips. Finally, gather a few strips together and cut into tiny cubes. Divide the beef between four plates, spreading out the meat into a rough circle. Cover closely with cling film and refridgerate until ready to serve.

5. When ready to go, heat the oven to its hottest setting (220°C/fan 200°C/gas mark 7) and put in two baking sheets to get blazing hot. Carefully put the pitta rounds onto the hot baking sheets and bake for 6–10 minutes, until puffed up and beginning to colour.

6. Remove the cling film from the meat and dot with the curd cheese, capers and parsley. Drizzle each plate with about a tablespoon of olive oil and a pinch of sea salt.

7. Serve the pitta bread with the steak tartare the minute the pitta is done.

A blob of good homemade mayonnaise could replace the olive oil.

I've made tartare with lamb, duck breast and even ostrich fillet – all good – but a traditional breed of British beef like Dexter or Aberdeen Angus is still the best.

Burrata with kumquats, coriander and lavender

Serves 4

For the kumquats

140g granulated sugar

1 small red chilli, halved lengthways and deseeded

2 flower heads of fresh lavender or 1 tsp dried lavender petals

250g kumquats

4 sprigs of coriander, leaves picked

For the burrata

1 tbsp coriander seeds

4 small burrata

2 flower heads of fresh lavender

sea salt flakes

I really disapprove of cookery writers stealing other writers' recipes wholesale. Of course, there are only so many ways to make a hollandaise sauce or a shepherd's pie. But when someone has a truly original idea, such as at Nopi restaurant, where they serve divine burrata with lavender-flavoured olive oil alongside slices of blood orange, then the least I can do is pay homage. It got me experimenting, and this is the happy result.

1. First make the syrup for the kumquats. In a heavy-based saucepan, heat the sugar in 285ml water with the chilli and lavender until dissolved, then add the kumquats and cook very gently for 20 minutes so the kumquats soften without exploding. Lift them out with a slotted spoon and set aside. Continue to simmer the syrup for 20–30 minutes until reduced to the consistency of runny honey. Discard the flower heads.

2. Meanwhile, for the burrata, toss the coriander seeds in a small dry pan over high heat for about 2 minutes, until toasted.

3. Place a burrata on each plate, then spoon 4–5 kumquats alongside. Spoon over some of the chilli syrup and scatter with coriander leaves.

4. Remove a few lavender petals from the bottom half of each flower head, then discard the head and stems. Scatter the petals over the burrata with the coriander seeds and sea salt.

A whole burrata for each person looks great on the plate and is so delicious it will certainly get eaten. But if you are doing this for a dinner-party starter, make sure you follow it with something light. Otherwise, halve the burratas.

In the absence of fresh lavender, dried will do, but don't use more than a teaspoon in the syrup and don't sprinkle any on top.

Roasted cauliflower and turmeric on rye

Serves 6

6 tbsp olive oil

1 large cauliflower (about 700g), leaves trimmed

8cm (3in) piece of fresh turmeric, peeled

3 garlic cloves, finely sliced

2 tsp brown sugar

1 x 400g tin butter beans, drained

juice an d finely grated zest of 1 large lemon

6 sprigs of coriander plus extra to garnish

salt and pepper to season

To serve

6 slices of light rye bread

1–2 tbsp olive oil

1 large garlic clove, halved

100g full-fat Greek yoghurt

Fresh turmeric is now available in good supermarkets, and it's worth getting if you can. Otherwise, use about 2 teaspoons ground dried turmeric.

1. Heat the oven to 200°C/fan 180°C/gas mark 6. Use 1 tablespoon of the oil to grease a large roasting tin.

2. Divide the cauliflower into small florets, not much bigger than 4–5cm (1½ in). Remove the large, central stalk. Tip the florets into the roasting tin and grate over the turmeric. Add the garlic, brown sugar and half the remaining olive oil and mix well. Season with salt and pepper. Roast in the oven for 15 minutes until the cauliflower florets are a turmeric yellow and nearly tender. Add the butter beans, lemon juice and the remaining olive oil. Shake the tin to roll the beans about so they get coated in the juices and return to the oven for a further 10 minutes. Remove from the oven and stir through the coriander.

3. Rub each slice of rye bread with a cut side of the garlic clove. Heat the olive oil in a medium frying pan over a medium heat. Add the garlicky slices of bread to the pan and fry for 2–3 minutes, turning once or twice, until slightly crisp. Transfer to serving plates and top with a spoonful of the cauliflower mixture. Sprinkle on the lemon zest and coriander. Add a spoonful of yoghurt to each plate.

Another version of this dish makes a great vegetarian main course. Instead of cutting the cauliflower into small florets, cut it into 'steaks' by slicing it thickly like a loaf of bread. You will need a small cauli for two people. Only the middle bits, with a lot of stalk, will be 'steaks', but the end florets need not be wasted. Roast the steaks and stray florets as above, adding the beans halfway through the cooking. Serve warm or cold, without the bread.

Fresh apple, fennel and feta salad

Serves 4

1 tbsp olive oil

6 rashers of streaky bacon

75g walnuts, roughly chopped

2 green apples, such as Granny Smith

1 small fennel bulb

75g green (or golden) raisins

a small handful of coriander leaves, finely chopped

175g block of feta, cut into 4 squares

For the dressing

juice of 1 lemon

1 garlic clove, crushed

4 tbsp extra virgin olive oil

a pinch of caster sugar

salt and pepper

This is one of those simple, but totally satisfactory salads. The sour apple, salty feta and sweet raisins work like a dream. Omit the bacon for a veggie version.

1. Heat the olive oil in a large, heavy-based frying pan over a high heat. Add the bacon and fry until crisp. Drain on kitchen paper and chop or scrunch into smaller, bite-sized pieces. Wipe the pan clean and dry-fry the walnuts over a medium heat, until just toasted. Remove and set aside.

2. Core and halve the apples. Cut into thin slices and then into fine matchsticks. Cut the base from the fennel bulb. Use a mandoline or your finest knife skills to cut the fennel into paper-thin slices. Mix the apple and fennel with the raisins, coriander and half the walnuts.

3. Put the dressing ingredients into a big bowl and whisk until smooth and combined. Pour over the salad and gently toss. Divide between four plates and top with a square of feta, the pieces of bacon and the remaining walnuts.

Look for green raisins in Lebanese shops. Golden ones are more easily available, but, frankly, any raisins or sultanas will do.

Ajiaco – Colombian chicken and potato soup

Serves 8

1 x 1.65–1.8kg chicken

2 litres hot chicken stock

2 garlic cloves, crushed

500g small new or salad potatoes, scrubbed and cut into quarters

3 Maris Piper potatoes, peeled and thinly sliced

a small teacup of dried guascas leaves

3 corn-on-the-cobs, each cut into 3 chunks

4 spring onions, finely sliced

a handful of coriander leaves, finely chopped

salt and pepper to season

To serve

175ml double cream

½ jar small capers, rinsed well and drained

1–2 ripe avocados, sliced

Ajiaco is a wonderful one-course meal. As you'd expect, it has typical South American ingredients: corn, avocado, two kinds of potato. It's easy to make, looks lovely, is healthy, and none of your friends will have heard of it. The only downside is that the distinctive flavour, which is just perfect, comes from a common Colombian herb called guascas, which you won't find in any supermarket. Since it's what makes the soup taste Colombian it's worth getting online from La Chatica Deli Shop (lachaticadeli.com). But if you can't get guascas, it's not the end of the world. I have made it with fresh coriander and with fresh basil and both were very good.

1. Put the chicken in a large saucepan with the stock and the garlic. Bring to a simmer. Then cook, without letting it boil, for about 50 minutes or until the chicken thigh feels tender when pierced and the leg will wobble. Lift out the chicken and set aside. When it's cool enough to handle, remove the skin and bones and cut the flesh into large chunks (use a sharp knife and cut the breast against the grain – don't shred into stringy bits). Cover the chicken with an upturned bowl while you continue with the soup.

2. Add both types of potato and the guascas to the stock. Simmer until the Maris Piper potatoes are breaking up, about 20 minutes. Then add the corn chunks and cook for 10 more minutes. Add the spring onions and chopped coriander. Taste and add salt and black pepper to taste. Return the chicken to the pan and gently reheat.

3. Serve each person, making sure everyone gets broth, chicken, corn and potato. Serve the ajiaco with cream, capers and avocado slices on the side.

Baked sea bass
with samphire and cucumber

Serves 2

1 lemon, sliced

1 whole sea bass
(500–600g), cleaned

½ leek or 2 shallots,
finely sliced

1 red chilli, deseeded
and finely sliced

2–3 stems of flat-leaf
parsley, finely chopped

a glass of tart white wine

a glug of olive oil

salt and pepper to season

For the salad

½ cucumber

100g samphire

1 tbsp olive oil

40g butter

2 garlic cloves, crushed

5–6 radishes, finely sliced

a small handful of dill
fronds

juice and finely grated zest
of 1 lemon

This works well with sea bream too. There's something festive and exciting about the sight of a whole fish arriving at the table. Use a good knife in one hand and a flat fish slice in the other to lift the pieces of fillet, skin and all (some of us love the skin!), from the backbone.

1. Heat the oven to 200°C/fan 180°C/gas mark 6.

2. Arrange the lemon slices in an oiled baking tray and lay the fish on top. Stuff the cavity with the leek or shallots, chilli and parsley. Trickle the wine over the fish, along with a good drizzle of olive oil. Season with salt and black pepper, then cover the tray tightly with foil and bake for 15–20 minutes, until a skewer glides easily through the side of the fish.

3. For the salad, prepare the cucumber by cutting it in half lengthways and scooping out the seeds with a teaspoon, leaving you with a 'cucumber boat'. Slice finely, on the diagonal, to produce crescent shapes. Set aside while you make the rest of the salad.

4. Wash the samphire in cold running water and trim off any tough ends. Heat the olive oil and butter in a large frying pan over a medium heat and add the garlic. Fry for a minute before adding the samphire and tossing it in the garlic butter. Cook for 2–3 minutes, until just soft, before removing from the heat and emptying into a bowl, along with the garlicky butter from the pan. Add the cucumber, radishes, dill, and lemon juice and zest. Toss to combine and check the seasoning, adjusting if needed.

5. Use two fish slices to lift the cooked fish onto a serving plate. As you dish up, spoon some salad onto the plates with the fish.

Samphire is also known as sea asparagus, perhaps because they share the same season (spring) but samphire can be harder to find. If you have trouble sourcing it, asparagus will do just fine.

Andhra fish curry

Serves 6

75g dried tamarind pulp

100ml sunflower oil

2 onions, finely chopped

1 tsp fenugreek seeds

1 tsp black mustard seeds

½ tsp cumin seeds

¼ tsp salt

2 garlic cloves, finely sliced

1 green chilli, finely sliced

3 tsp Andhra curry powder
(or 2 tsp Kashmiri chilli
powder and 1 tsp ground
turmeric)

1 mango cheek from a large
unripe mango or 1 whole
small unripe mango

450g ripe tomatoes,
chopped, or 1 x 400g tin
chopped tomatoes

about 6 curry leaves,
fresh or dried

500g haddock fillet, skinned
and cut into bite-sized
chunks

140g long-grain rice

3 spring onions, chopped

a small handful of fresh
coriander leaves

Andhra curry powder is made using Kashmiri chilli powder, which comes from deep red, dried chillies with wrinkled skin. It imparts a vibrant red colour and a mild heat. If you can't get it, use two-thirds Kashmiri chilli powder with one-third turmeric.

This is a tomato-based fish curry that, unusually, doesn't use coconut milk – the distinct tastes come from Kashmiri chilli powder, tamarind and mango, but the spices and flavourings give a subtle and layered flavour. Haddock keeps its texture and flavour well, as does cod. I have also made it with pollock, which is generally a pretty flavour-free fish, but takes these flavours really well.

1. Start by boiling 150ml water and submerging the tamarind in it. Leave to soak for at least 15 minutes.

2. Heat the oil in a deep saucepan or flameproof casserole over a medium heat and fry the onions, fenugreek, mustard and cumin seeds with the salt. When the onions are soft, add the garlic, green chilli, curry powder or chilli powder and turmeric. Cook for a further minute or so.

3. Cut the flesh from the mango, but leave the skin on. Then slice the flesh crossways, trying to ensure that each slice has a strip of peel. Add these slices, the tomatoes and the curry leaves to the pan and cook, covered, for 10 minutes, until the tomatoes are soft. Strain the tamarind pulp through a sieve, pressing down with the back of a spoon to get all but the seeds through. Pour the liquid into the curry.

4. Rinse the rice in cold water. Put into a saucepan, pour over enough water to cover by 2–3cm (1in) and bring to a boil. Cover and reduce the heat to a simmer. Cook for roughly 10 minutes without lifting the lid, until the rice is tender. Remove from the heat and set aside, still covered, until ready to be served.

5. Return the curry to a simmer for a minute or two (it should be liquid, but thick) before adding the fish and cooking for 4 minutes. Turn off the heat and let the haddock continue to cook gently in the curry for a few minutes while the flavour penetrates the fish.

6. Tip the curry into a serving dish and garnish with the spring onions and coriander. Serve with the rice.

Autumn mackerel

Serves 4

4 beetroot, scrubbed clean and cut into 2cm (¾ in) cubes

3 garlic cloves, finely sliced

2 tbsp peeled and finely grated fresh horseradish

4 tbsp olive oil plus extra for brushing and for dressing

160g green lentils

2–3 tbsp red wine vinegar

a small bunch of chives, finely chopped

4 fresh mackerel fillets

1 head of red chicory

1 lemon, cut into wedges

salt and pepper to season

Mackerel is the most flavourful of fish, but it has to be really fresh. Better buy frozen mackerel fillets from a supermarket than tired-looking fish, with their skins dull instead of iridescent, from a fishmonger. But if you see fresh mackerel with shiny skin and eyes not sunken, then pounce on them, buying more than you need if you can. Get the fishmonger to fillet them for you, then freeze whatever you don't need.

1. Heat the oven to 200°C/fan 180°C/gas mark 6.

2. Put the beetroot, garlic and horseradish into a large roasting tin. Drizzle over half the olive oil, season well and mix. Roast for 25 minutes or until tender, giving everything a good stir halfway through.

3. Cook the lentils for 15–20 minutes in a large saucepan of salted boiling water or until just tender. Drain and return to the pan. Add the roasted beetroot, the remaining olive oil, the red wine vinegar and half the chives.

4. Heat the grill until blazing-hot. With a razor-sharp knife, make three diagonal cuts through the skin of each mackerel fillet, taking care not to go deeply into the flesh. Brush with olive oil and dust with a little salt and black pepper. Lay them, skin side up, on a sheet of oiled foil on the grill pan. When the grill is hot, slide the fish under it, and grill for 3–4 minutes until the skin is beginning to brown and crisp. Remove the fillets from the pan.

5. Meanwhile, dress the chicory leaves with a touch of olive oil, salt and pepper.

6. To serve, spoon a portion of beetroot and lentils onto each plate and add a few dressed chicory leaves. Top with the mackerel, then garnish with chives and a lemon wedge.

Salmon in pastry with curried eggs and spinach filling

2 x 500g blocks of puff
pastry

2 x 600g sides of salmon
(kept whole, skinned and
boned)

140g large spinach or
kale leaves

4 tbsp flat-leaf parsley
leaves, chopped

2 tsp mild curry paste

4 hard-boiled medium
eggs, chopped

2 tbsp semolina

1 beaten egg for glazing

salt and pepper to season

watercress and mustard
to serve (optional)

(Pictured overleaf.)

**This is a take on the classic salmon en croute, the difference being the
addition of a curried egg and spinach filling. It looks complicated but is
easy to do if you follow the recipe word for word. If you are a hot-stuff
pastry cook, you can of course make your own puff pastry, which is fun
and satisfying to do. I've not included the recipe here, though, because
I suspect, like me, you'll be buying it ready-made.**

**Apologies right at the start! You really only need about 750g ready-
made puff pastry but it comes in 500g blocks so you are going to be
left with about half a block. Cut it off before you begin and freeze it
for another time.**

1. Heat the oven to 220°C/fan 200°C/gas mark 6.

2. Cut one pastry block in half (and freeze the rest) and roll out thinly
into a strip roughly the same length and half the width of the salmon
fillet. Put the strip of pastry on a flat baking sheet (or the back of a baking
tray) and cover with a second baking sheet (to stop it rising too much).
Bake for 18–20 minutes, until it is a good, deep brown. Remove from the
baking sheets and allow to cool.

3. Make sure the salmon fillets have no bones. (Feel along the flesh with
your fingers to locate any stray pinbones and pull them out with your
fingers or cook's tweezers).

4. Cut out the tough stalks of the spinach or kale with scissors (if you
fold each leaf in half along the stalk, it's easy). Bring a wide pan of water
to the boil, drop in the leaves and hold them under water with a fish slice
until they are limp and wilted. Drain off the hot water and replace with
cold. Repeat until both the water and spinach are cold. Carefully lift out
the spinach leaves and lay down on a clean tea towel to dry.

5. Mix the parsley, curry paste and eggs together. Season well with salt
and black pepper.

6. Lay the cooked pastry rectangle in the middle of a board and sprinkle with the semolina. Lay half the wilted spinach or kale leaves over the semolina and cover with a fillet of salmon. Pile on the egg mixture and put the other salmon fillet on top to make a sandwich. (Try to match the thick side of the top fillet to the thin side of the bottom one to end up with a more-or-less-level top surface.) Cover with the remaining wilted spinach or kale leaves. Pat dry with kitchen paper or a clean tea towel.

7. Roll out the second pastry block into a thin sheet large enough to wrap the salmon: your rectangle needs to be roughly four times the width of your salmon sandwich and 8cm (3in) longer. Drape the sheet of pastry over the salmon, tucking the edges under and using a fish slice to lift the roll a bit as you tuck.

8. Roll out any pastry trimmings to use as decoration (resist the temptation to screw it up into a ball because that will destroy the layers that puff up so nicely when cooking.) Embellish the top with pastry leaves or fish shapes made from the trimmings, or score fine lines with the back of a knife. Carefully transfer the salmon to a baking sheet and brush the whole thing with beaten egg.

9. Bake for 25–30 minutes or until the pastry is brown and a skewer will penetrate the salmon sandwich easily. Allow to cool a little before slicing. This is good hot or cold, served with salad.

> The idea of including semolina and a cooked pastry layer is to absorb some of the cooking juices and so prevent a soggy bottom.
>
> If you only have a baking tray with raised sides, use the back of it. Then you can slide your finished creation straight onto a serving dish rather than risk cracking it as you lift it over the edge of the tray.

Pan-fried halibut
with green spaghetti

Serves 2

150g spaghetti or linguine

200g kale, tough stalks
removed

4 garlic cloves, peeled and
left whole

100g baby spinach or large
leaves, stalks removed

about 2 tbsp olive oil

30g Parmesan cheese,
finely grated

salt and pepper to season

For the halibut

2 x 225g halibut steaks,
skin on

a good glug of olive oil

juice of ½ lemon plus lemon
wedges to serve

Good fresh halibut of a decent thickness is expensive and hard to find, especially if you are rightly avoiding unsustainable fish. But it is the king of fish, with no small bones, firm white flesh, and it tastes unbelievably good – so good that it's best with minimum complication.

The idea of colouring pasta is hardly new. Cooks have used spinach, beetroot and saffron to turn it green, red or yellow for generations. But I was intrigued by Jamie Oliver's use of kale to colour pasta, then make a green sauce with it, so I've stolen the idea. Spinach works as well as kale, and you get the best flavour and colour with a bit of both.

1. Bring a deep saucepan of water to the boil, salt generously, then add the spaghetti and boil for 4 minutes before adding the kale and garlic cloves. After 2 minutes add the spinach and continue to cook for a further 4 minutes. Use tongs to remove the spinach and kale from the water, setting them aside. Taste the pasta. When it is just cooked (it should be al dente) then strain it, keeping half a cupful of cooking water for the sauce. Use a slotted poon to fish out the garlic cloves and add them to the spinach and kale. Return the spaghetti to the still-hot saucepan and stir through a teaspoon or two of the olive oil to prevent it sticking.

2. Pour the rest of the olive oil into a liquidizer and add the hot spinach, kale and garlic, plus enough of the cooking water to make a smooth, thickish sauce. Blend, then add the Parmesan, taste and season well. Stir the sauce through the pasta and cover to keep warm while you fry the halibut.

3. Season the halibut steaks on both sides. Heat the olive oil in a heavy-based frying pan until smoking hot. Add the steaks and fry until the undersides are golden brown, pressing the fish lightly with the back of a spatula to get an even colour. Avoid moving the fish around (don't look for the first 3 minutes, then carefully lift the steaks and check). When brown, turn over and cook the other side for 3 minutes. Squeeze over the lemon juice and taste to check the seasoning. Remove from the pan and dish up with the pasta and lemon wedges.

My Lebanese table

(All pictured on pages 174–75.)

I had a Lebanese sister-in-law and she made these dishes all the time: batata harra, tabbouleh, mujadera served with the soft cheese labne. She would serve them as mezze with drinks, as salads or as accompaniments to meat dishes, but I liked them best (and still do) eaten together as a healthy vegetarian meal. What started as a combination of leftovers has become my preferred meal. If you omit the labne, you have a great vegan meal. All of these benefit from serving with freshly baked pitta bread (see pages 148–49).

Batata harra

Serves 4 as part of a main course, 8 as part of my table

about 4 tbsp good olive oil

750g potatoes, peeled and cut into 1.5cm (¾ in) cubes

1 small red chilli, deseeded and finely sliced

3 large garlic cloves, finely sliced

3 sprigs of coriander, chopped

salt and pepper to season

This is one of the most delicious ways to cook potatoes. A bit more trouble than boiling or roasting, but absolutely worth it.

1. Heat the oil in a large frying pan over a gentle heat. Add the potatoes and fry very slowly, shaking the pan and turning the cubes until pale brown on all sides. Add the chilli and garlic and continue frying gently until the garlic is just turning colour and the potatoes are evenly browned.

2. Add the coriander, season with salt and pepper and serve hot.

Tabbouleh

Serves 4 as part of a
main course, 8 as part
of my table

100g bulgur wheat

3 large handfuls of flat-leaf
parsley

2 sprigs of fresh mint, leaves
picked

1 large tomato, finely diced

juice and finely grated zest
of 2 lemons

salt and pepper to season

Tabbouleh is unusual in that its main ingredient is parsley. I use the flat-leafed rather than the curly variety, which is a bit scratchy unless you chop it really finely. It's served mixed with a little cracked wheat (bulgur or burghul), which, being broken into small bits, needs no lengthy soaking or boiling. Tabbouleh usually has a little finely chopped tomato in it and always has a good deal of sharp fresh lemon juice. You can add diced cucumber too (see Tip below) or a dash of olive oil, but this recipe is tabbouleh at its simplest.

1. Pour boiling water over the bulgur wheat, leave for a few minutes, then drain. Dry the wheat by squeezing it in a clean tea towel.

2. Chop the parsley stalks finely and the leaves more coarsely. Tear or chop up the mint leaves.

3. Mix all the ingredients together, taste and check the seasoning.

> If you want a milder, less parsley-dominated salad, cucumber is a good addition. Cut the cucumber into the smallest dice you can, skin and all, then sprinkle with salt, which will draw out the juices. (If you don't do this, you must add the cucumber at the very last minute or the salt in the tabbouleh will draw out the cucumber liquid, making the salad wet and soggy.) After half an hour, rinse the cucumber under the cold tap and dry on a clean tea towel before adding to the salad.

Mujadera

Serves 4 as part of a
main course, 8 as part
of my table

150g brown lentils

½ tsp salt

75g basmati rice

2 large onions, finely sliced

3 tbsp olive oil

2 large garlic cloves, crushed

salt and pepper to season

Mujadera, being a traditional peasant dish, is never served in smart restaurants, but it's cooked in every Lebanese home kitchen. It's so simple: basically a dish of lentils and rice with crisply fried onions. You can spice it up if you like, with cinnamon and allspice as I have here, or with cumin, turmeric or chilli. But I also love it unspiced, with just a heavy hit of garlic. And who doesn't like crisp fried onions?

1. Put the lentils in a medium-sized saucepan and cover with 200ml water. Add the salt and simmer gently for 10 minutes, until softened but not cooked through. Add the rice and a further 200ml water. Put a lid on the pan and simmer for roughly 10 minutes, or until the rice is cooked, by which time the lentils will be too, and the water almost all absorbed. Set aside with the lid on.

2. Fry the onions in the oil over medium-high heat, stirring frequently to prevent them burning, until they are brown and some are beginning to crisp at the edges. This will take about 10 minutes. Add the garlic and keep frying for a minute.

3. The rice and lentils should now have absorbed all the water. If they haven't, drain off the excess and then shake the pan over the heat to steam dry the contents. Spoon half the fried onions into the pan. Taste and season with salt and pepper.

4. Tip the mujadera into a serving bowl and keep warm. Just before serving, top with the reserved fried onions.

Labne

½ tsp salt

500g good-quality full-fat yoghurt

olive oil, to store

1. Stir the salt through the yoghurt. Line a sieve with a piece of muslin that's large enough to overhang the sieve. Spoon the yoghurt into it. Bring the overhanging muslin together over the top to cover the yoghurt completely.

2. Leave to drip into a bowl or over the sink for 24 hours, or until the yoghurt has drained sufficiently to thicken to a spreadable consistency. It is now a fresh cheese.

3. Roll the cheese into balls, roughly 20g each. Gently lower them into a clean jar, then carefully pour olive oil over the cheese to cover. The labne can be eaten immediately or stored submerged in the olive oil for up to 3 months.

Before storing in olive oil, or just before serving, you can roll the labne balls in chopped herbs, like rosemary or basil, or in coarsely ground spices like black pepper or coriander, or in dried chilli flakes or paprika.

If you don't have any muslin, a clean rinsed-out J-cloth will do fine.

Spicy Middle Eastern lamb meatballs with giant couscous

2 tsp cumin seeds

2 tsp coriander seeds

½ tsp ground cinnamon

500g lamb mince

½ small red chilli, deseeded and finely diced

20g dried breadcrumbs

1–2 stems of mint, leaves picked and finely chopped, plus extra leaves to garnish

finely grated zest of 1 lemon

3 tablespoons vegetable oil

salt and pepper to season

1 onion, finely chopped

2 garlic cloves, sliced

1 tsp ground cumin

2 tbsp tomato purée

2 x 400g tins chopped tomatoes

1 x 400g tin kidney beans, drained and rinsed

200g giant couscous

1 tbsp olive oil

2 tbsp flaked almonds, toasted

pomegranate seeds to serve

I think these are the best lamb meatballs I've ever made, flavoured with toasted coriander seeds and fresh chilli. But almost all meatballs are good, and it's worth experimenting. Just remember that breadcrumbs make the meatballs softer; that the leaner the meat, the drier the meatballs will be (fat in the mix enhances the flavour); and that if the meat is from a 'grilling' cut (i.e. tender enough to fry or barbecue), you can eat the meatballs as soon as they are fried, but if you are using 'stewing' meat, they will need longer cooking in a sauce or in the oven.

The best way to get the spicing to your liking is to fry a teaspoon of the mix, then taste and keep adding more of whatever you think it needs until you have the perfect flavour.

1. Toast the cumin and coriander seeds in a frying pan over a medium heat until fragrant, then crush to a powder in a pestle and mortar. Stir through the cinnamon.

2. Put the mince, spices, chilli, breadcrumbs, mint and lemon zest in a large bowl. Use your hands to mix everything really thoroughly. Season well and taste (see note in the introduction above if you don't want to taste it raw). Shape into twelve balls, each the size of a golf ball.

3. Heat the vegetable oil in a deep, heavy-based frying pan over a medium heat. Add the meatballs in batches and cook for 5–6 minutes, shaking the pan gently, and turning carefully to brown them evenly all over. Remove from the pan and set aside while you make the sauce.

4. Wipe out the frying pan and add a glug more oil, then add the onion. Stir until it begins to colour, then add the garlic and cumin. Cook for a minute, then add the tomato purée. Turn up the heat to high and add the tomatoes. Cook for 15 minutes, until the sauce has thickened, stirring occasionally. Mix in the kidney beans before nestling in the meatballs. Cover and simmer for 20 minutes or until the meatballs are tender.

5. Put a large saucepan of salted water on to boil. Add the couscous and boil for 15–18 minutes or until tender, but still with a little bite. Drain under warm water, then tip into a bowl and gently toss with the olive oil.

6. Sprinkle the meatballs with toasted almonds, pomegranate seeds and the extra mint leaves. Serve with the giant couscous.

Fast-roast teriyaki lamb

Serves 4–6

1kg (de-boned weight)
whole leg of lamb,
open-boned

1 tbsp olive oil

300ml teriyaki sauce or
dark soy sauce

2 tbsp runny honey

salt to season

coriander leaves to garnish

I like this recipe because it's a foolproof way of getting meat perfectly rare for a tableful of guests. Just make a timetable and stick it on the fridge door. Turn the oven on half an hour before your guests are due to arrive. When the last guest arrives, put the lamb in the oven before opening the front door. Join the guests for a drink. Half an hour later, take the lamb out, and set aside to rest. Serve the first course. When the first course is over, serve the lamb. No need to make gravy, either – the juices and the teriyaki do that. The lamb can be a whole boned, opened-out shoulder if you prefer: the cooking times will be the same (it is the thickness, not the weight, that determines cooking time).

Ask your butcher to open-bone or 'butterfly' a leg of lamb. Tell them you want to end up with about a kilo of boneless meat.

1. Have a look at your lamb. If the butcher has done a good job, the meat should be of a pretty even thickness. If one side is thicker than the other, that side will be rarer when cooked. But someone always prefers rare meat, so don't worry. With a very sharp knife (or Stanley knife), lightly score the skin side of the lamb in a criss-cross pattern.

2. Put the lamb in a big flat container greased with the olive oil. Rub half the teriyaki or soy sauce and all the honey all over it. Cover and leave in the fridge to marinate overnight, or for at least a few hours. Take it out of the fridge for the last hour to bring it to room temperature before cooking.

3. Heat the oven to 240°C/fan 220°C/gas mark 9.

4. Sprinkle the lamb with salt and transfer it, together with its marinade, into a roasting tin. Roast for 25 minutes for rare, 30 for medium and 35 for well done. (Add 5 minutes to the roasting times if the boned lamb weighs more than 1.5kg.)

5. Lift the lamb out of its tin onto a carving board or dish and allow to rest under foil and a tea towel for 20 minutes.

6. Add the rest of the teriyaki or soy to the roasting juices in the tin, along with any juices that have run out of the lamb as it rested. Reheat and tip into a jug.

7. Slice and serve with a spoonful of the juices, garnished with coriander.

Slow-roast shoulder of lamb with anchovy

Serves 6 generously

1 shoulder of lamb, bone in (about 2.5kg)

2 x 50g tins anchovy fillets in oil (60g drained weight)

2 red onions, each cut into 6 segments

2 large carrots, sliced into 2.5cm (1in) rounds

3 or 4 sprigs of rosemary

2 x 400g tins chopped tomatoes

2–3 fresh bay leaves

500ml red wine

salt and pepper to season

1 celeriac (about 900g), peeled and cut into 3–4cm (1½ in) cubes

1 Maris Piper potato (about 175g), peeled and cut into 3–4cm (1½ in) cubes

75ml whole milk

40g butter

To serve

a handful of peeled pistachios, roughly chopped

a handful of flat-leaf parsley leaves, roughly chopped

This recipe couldn't be easier. Just a question of putting all the ingredients in a large roasting tin and letting the oven do the work. When cooked, the lamb should be so tender that it can be pulled apart with a fork. Serve with celeriac mash to make the whole thing into a feast.

1. Heat the oven to 170°C/fan 150°C/gas mark 3.

2. Prepare the lamb by removing any excess fat and using a sharp knife or Stanley knife to score a criss-cross pattern in the skin. Put the anchovy fillets and half their oil into a food processer or blender and blitz. Rub this paste over the skin side of the lamb.

3. Put the onions, carrots, rosemary, tomatoes and bay leaves into a roasting tin and nestle the lamb shoulder on top. Pour the red wine into the tin. Season with black pepper.

4. Cover with a sheet of baking parchment and then one of foil, tucking it round the edges of the tin to keep the steam in. Bake in the oven for about 5–6 hours, basting the meat every other hour. The lamb is ready when the meat is falling away from the bone. Skim off the fat using a large spoon.

5. Put the celeriac and potato into a large saucepan with a good sprinkling of salt. Cover with water and boil until tender. Drain, and toss in the pan for a minute to steam dry, then mash with a hand masher.

6. Once the mash is smooth, push it to the side of the saucepan and set over a medium heat. Pour the milk into the pan, next to the mash, and add the butter. Once the milk is hot, mix it into the mash.

7. Serve the lamb (which should be wonderfully tender and fall to pieces) on a bed of mash, sprinkled with pistachios and chopped parsley.

Potatoes go famously gluey when 'mashed' in a food processor, or even if beaten too vigorously by hand, but you could use the food processor for this mash. It only has one potato, and that's a well-behaved Maris Piper, and a lot of celeriac, which never goes gloopy.

Roast pork with crackling and apple sauce

Serves 10

2.3kg boned loin of pork, with skin on

2 tsp cooking oil

1 tbsp plain flour

425ml good stock

salt and pepper to season

a small bunch of watercress to garnish

mustard to serve

For the apple sauce

450g Bramley apples, peeled, cored and sliced

2–3 tbsp sugar

It really pays to spend money on good pork. There is all the difference in the world between meat from an old-fashioned pig like a Middle White or Gloucester Old Spot that has been allowed to rootle about outdoors, and a pallid joint from a barn-reared beast fed on pellets. You need a good butcher too! The most maddening thing for a cook is to get a beautiful joint of pork with a few vandal's slashes through the skin instead of perfectly scored crackling. If your butcher or the supermarket do not know how to do it properly, do it yourself. It's easy!

1. Heat the oven to 220°C/fan 200°C/gas mark 7.

2. Score the pork rind for crackling: using a Stanley knife or a very sharp knife, make long fine cuts through the skin into the fat, but not through the fat into the flesh. The cuts need to be really close together, not more than a pencil's width apart and completely cover the skin.

3. Oil the palm of your hand and rub it all over the pork skin. Put the joint into a roasting tin and, once the oven is hot (not before), sprinkle the skin all over with a good dusting of salt. (It's the salt that makes the skin bubble up instead of cooking to inedible leather.) Roast the joint in the middle of the oven for an hour, then turn the oven down to 190°C/fan 170°C/gas mark 5 and roast for a further hour.

4. For the apple sauce, put the apple slices in a pan with 100ml water and the sugar. Cook slowly, covered, until the apples are soft. Beat briefly and tip into a serving bowl. Set aside.

5. Test the pork for 'doneness' by piercing the meat with a skewer (not through the crackling). The juices should run out clear. If they are pink, return the roast to the oven and cook for a further 15 minutes, then test again. Once cooked, put the pork on a serving dish and turn off the oven. Allow the joint to cool for 10 minutes, then place in the still-warm oven.

6. Tip off all but a tablespoon of the fat from the roasting tin. Set the tin over a medium heat and stir the flour into the remaining fat and juices, scraping up the stuck bits as you do so. When the flour has browned, add the stock and whisk constantly while bringing to the boil. Simmer for a few minutes until the gravy is shiny and slightly thickened. Season to taste. Strain into a warmed jug. Garnish the pork with watercress and serve with the gravy, apple sauce and mustard.

Leith's roast duck

Serves 2

2 duck breasts

salt and pepper to season

For the sauce

15g butter

1 celery stick, finely
chopped

1 small onion, finely
chopped

30g granulated sugar

1 tbsp white wine vinegar

150ml strong poultry stock

finely grated zest and juice
of 1 orange

2 tsp brandy

To serve

45g flaked almonds, toasted

a bunch of watercress

This is based on my signature dish at Leith's Restaurant when we opened in 1969. It was so popular that it stayed on the menu for twenty-five years, until I sold the restaurant. At one point I thought the sixty-odd ducks we sold a week would justify me starting a duck farm, but then, did I really want a duck farm? No.

We used to roast the birds whole and the waiters would expertly carve them at the table. But for ease and speed I've adapted the recipe for duck breasts here, which also means you can cook the meat as rare as each of your diners prefers.

1. Heat the oven to 220°C/fan 200°C/gas mark 6.

2. Rub the duck breasts all over with sea salt and cracked black pepper. Lay them, skin side down, in a cold, heavy-based frying pan and set over a low heat. As the duck breast cooks, the fat will render and can be poured out into a bowl (to be used for roasting potatoes at a later date). After 10 minutes or so, the skin should be crisp and golden. Turn the breasts over and transfer to a small ovenproof dish or roasting tin.

3. Pour any fat out of the frying pan and discard. Wipe the pan clean, add the butter and return it to the heat. Once the butter is hot, fry the celery and onion for 4–5 minutes, stirring, until softened. Set aside.

4. Meanwhile, put the sugar and vinegar into a small, clean saucepan. Dissolve the sugar over a low heat, then boil until the sugar caramelizes: it should cook to a good deep brown, with large slow bubbles. Pour in the stock, which will hiss and splutter, so take care. Stir until the caramel lumps disappear. Add the softened celery and onion, followed by the orange zest and juice and the brandy. Spoon the sauce around the duck breasts and roast in the hot oven for 6–7 minutes.

5. Remove from the oven, cut into slices, and serve with a scattering of almonds and some watercress.

Lamb steaks Catalan with gremolata

Serves 4

3 garlic cloves, crushed

3 sprigs of rosemary, leaves picked and finely chopped

3 tbsp olive oil

salt and pepper to season

4 lamb steaks on the bone, about 1.5cm (¾ in) thick

vegetable oil for greasing

For the gremolata

2 tbsp flat-leaf parsley leaves, chopped

finely grated zest and juice of 1 lemon

2 fat garlic cloves, crushed

2 tbsp olive oil plus extra for greasing

½ tsp salt

½ tsp black pepper

Barbecue paradise, for me, consists of garlicky, slightly charred lamb steaks: heady with rosemary, sizzling on the outside and pink in the middle. But you can cook them on a really hot griddle or teppanyaki, or in a heavy frying pan. Get the butcher to cut the steaks from the heavy end of the leg, straight across the grain of the meat, either in round steaks with the bone in the middle, or half steaks without the bone. The main thing is that they should be at least half an inch thick.

1. Mix the garlic, rosemary, olive oil in a bowl, season with salt and pepper and add the lamb steaks. Cover the meat well and leave to marinate overnight or for at least an hour in the fridge.

2. Meanwhile, make the gremolata by simply combining the ingredients.

3. Dip a screw of kitchen paper in oil and use to grease a griddle pan or heavy frying pan. Get this really hot, then add the lamb steaks, along with any marinade that sticks to them. Griddle the steaks for 3–4 minutes without moving them (shifting them about spoils the griddle marks, and constantly lifting them to peer at the undersides allows them to cool and prevents them browning). When the tops of the steaks begin to look moist because the juices are being forced up through the meat, turn them over to grill the other side for a few minutes. If you want medium-rare meat, the steak should feel firm but not rigid when pressed with a finger or tongs.

4. Remove from the heat and allow to rest for a few minutes. Serve with the gremolata.

> If the lamb steaks are nice and thick and cut evenly, 3–4 minutes per side should give you a medium-rare steak. Allow 3 minutes per side for rare, and 6 minutes for well done. If well-done steaks are getting too brown, move them to the edge of the barbecue or lower the heat under the pan for the last minute or two on each side.

Peri-peri spatchcock chicken

Serves 6

For the peri-peri sauce

1 small red onion, roughly chopped

2 garlic cloves, chopped

1 large red chilli, stalk removed, roughly chopped

1 red pepper, cored deseeded, and roughly chopped

½ tsp mild chilli powder

2 tsp sugar

½ tsp paprika

1½ tbsp white wine vinegar

juice of 1 lemon

75ml olive oil

½ tsp salt

½ tsp black pepper

For the chicken

1 x 1.75kg chicken

1kg roasting potatoes, peeled and cut in half

1 tbsp olive oil

Most of the recipes in this book don't assume butchery skills, but it's really worth learning to spatchcock a chicken, which means opening it out flat. The bird will cook in half the time, and you get the legs crisp and brown as well as the breast. This sauce is easy to make, but here's a confession: I often use Nando's mild Peri Peri and everyone loves it.

If you don't have a rack to set over a roasting tin, grease the top oven rack in the middle and roast the chicken directly on that, putting the tin of potatoes to cook underneath.

1. Put all the sauce ingredients into a food processor and blitz.

2. Sit the bird breast-side down on a board. Using kitchen scissors, cut down one side of the backbone, cutting through the rib bones as you go. Cut down the other side of the backbone to remove it. Turn the bird over so the breast faces up and, using the heel of your hand, press down hard on the breastbone to flatten the bird. Trim off any fatty pieces around the tail. Use a cleaver or heavy knife to chop off the ends of the drumsticks and the wing tips, if you like. Now put a couple of skewers through the bird – one through the legs, one through the breast – to hold it flat.

3. Put the chicken in a shallow dish and add half the sauce. Spread over both sides of the chicken and leave in the fridge to marinate for as little as an hour, but preferably overnight.

4. Heat the oven to 200°C/fan 180°C/gas mark 6. In a large roasting tin, toss the potatoes in the olive oil and sprinkle lightly with the salt and pepper.

5. Set a greased wire rack over the roasting tin. Lift the chicken from the marinade and put it, skin-side down, onto the rack. Pour over any peri-peri sauce left behind in the dish and place the whole thing in the middle of the oven. Roast for 20 minutes.

6. Lift the chicken and its rack off the tin for a minute and set aside while you turn the potatoes to distribute the juices evenly. Turn the chicken over, so it's skin side up. Sprinkle with salt. Put everything back as before and roast for another 20–25 minutes, until the juices run clear when the thigh flesh is pierced with a skewer, and the skin is crispy and dark brown. Serve with the potatoes and the rest of the peri-peri sauce.

Chickpea, tomato
and sausage cassoulet

Serves 6

350g dried chickpeas,
soaked overnight, or
2 x 400g tins chickpeas,
drained

2 tbsp olive oil

8 Toulouse sausages

200g bacon, diced

2 onions, sliced

1 large carrot, peeled
and diced

1 celery stick, diced

4 garlic cloves, finely sliced

2 fresh bay leaves

4–5 sprigs of thyme, leaves
picked

3 tbsp tomato purée

6 ripe tomatoes, cut into
quarters

1 tbsp Worcestershire sauce

2 tbsp parsley leaves,
chopped

salt and pepper to season

Chickpeas, like most pulses, are wonderfully good at soaking up flavour. For this recipe, either use dried chickpeas and soak them overnight and then cook them a little longer, or use them straight out of the tin.

1. If using dried chickpeas that have been soaked, drain them and empty into a large, heavy-based saucepan. Cover with water and bring to a simmer. Cook for an hour, topping up the water if necessary, until the chickpeas are tender but still retain a slight bite. Drain and set aside. (If using tinned chickpeas, skip this step and just add them in at Step 3.)

2. Heat the olive oil in the same pan and set about browning the sausages and bacon. Fry until the sausages are brown on all sides and the bacon is really crisp. Remove from the pan and set aside. Add the onions, carrot and celery to the pan, with a touch more oil if necessary, and fry over a medium heat until softened, about 10 minutes. Stir constantly to prevent the vegetables catching. Add the garlic and continue to cook for a minute or two.

3. Return the sausage and bacon to the pan, along with the bay leaves, thyme, tomato purée, tomatoes and Worcestershire sauce. Gently stir together. Season really well, top up with fresh water (about 450ml), cover and simmer gently for 30 minutes. The beans will still be firm at this stage. (If using tinned chickpeas, add them now). Cover and cook for an hour. Check to make sure your cassoulet isn't drying out – add some hot water if needed. Remove from the heat and serve, garnished with parsley.

I love chickpeas, but other tinned beans work well here: kidney, borlotti, haricot. The only one I wouldn't recommend for this is the delicious butter bean, because it disintegrates so easily. But you could always cook the casserole without them, reheat them separately, and combine them gently at the last minute.

Monster sausage roll

(Pictured overleaf.)

There is nothing clever about this dish – it's just a jumbo sausage roll. But if you make your own filling, or better still make your own pastry and shape it into a fancy plait, and then serve it with a good homemade tomato sauce, it's pretty well irresistible.

Serves 6 generously

For the pastry

150g salted butter, frozen

220g plain flour

a good pinch of salt

For the filling

1 tbsp olive oil

2 banana shallots or
1 onion, finely chopped

2 garlic cloves, crushed

a small handful of sage
leaves, chopped

600g good-quality pork
sausagemeat, not too
finely minced

1 apple, grated

40g dried breadcrumbs

1 medium egg, beaten

salt and pepper to season

To bake

1 beaten egg for brushing

1 tsp fennel seeds to garnish

1. The butter needs to be very cold, so put it in the freezer for at least an hour before using.

2. For the pastry, put the flour and salt into a big bowl. Use the coarse side of a grater to grate long lengths of the frozen butter onto the flour. Mix with a palette knife or butter knife. Sprinkle 4 tablespoons cold water into the bowl and, still using the knife, mix until it begins to hold together. Quickly bring the pastry together with a floured hand, avoiding over-handling the dough. Add 1–2 tablespoons of water, if necessary, to bring it into a soft single lump. Shape into a flat rectangle about 1cm (½ in) thick. Wrap or cover in cling film and refrigerate for at least half an hour.

3. On to the filling. Heat the olive oil in a frying pan on a low heat and gently fry the shallots or onion until soft and translucent. Stir in the garlic and sage and cook for a further 2 minutes. Transfer to a bowl and allow to cool.

4. Add the remaining filling ingredients to the bowl and mix everything together well. Fry a teaspoonful, taste and add more seasoning or sage if necessary.

5. Heat the oven to 200°C/fan 180°C/gas mark 6.

6. On a floured surface, roll out the pastry to a large rectangle about 25cm x 35cm (10in x 14in). Trim the edges to make them dead straight. Shape the filling into a long 'sausage', 2cm (1in) shorter than the longest side of the pastry. Lay it along the centre of the pastry rectangle with the end of the sausage level with the bottom end of the pastry.

7. With a small sharp knife, cut the pastry on each side of the filling into parallel thin ribbons, like the teeth of a comb, but at a 30-degree angle.

8. Now bring a pastry ribbon from one side over the hump of the sausage, and then bring one from the other side over that. Repeat all the way down the sausage roll, using ribbons of pastry from alternate sides, until you have covered the whole sausage. Neaten up the pastry at the top and bottom of the roll, tucking the ends under. Freeze the sausage roll for 20 minutes or chill in the fridge for 40 minutes.

9. Transfer to a baking sheet and brush the with beaten egg. Sprinkle over the fennel seeds. Bake for 25 minutes, until puffed up and golden brown. Remove from the oven, then serve hot or cold, cut into slices.

If using ready-made pastry, I think puff works better here than shortcrust. And of course you don't have to go in for the fancy plaiting, but it's fun to do, and once you've done it once, and understand how to cut the pastry, it only takes a few minutes.

Serve the sausage roll with a green salad with a mustardy French dressing to make an excellent lunch or supper dish. Children love it.

Vinegar chicken

30g butter

1 tbsp cooking oil

8 chicken thighs or 4 whole legs, knuckles removed

5 large garlic cloves, unpeeled

150ml white wine vinegar

300ml dry white wine

2 tbsp brandy

2 tsp Dijon mustard

1 tbsp tomato purée

150ml double cream

salt and pepper to season

To serve

a handful of cashews, roughly chopped and toasted

1 large very ripe tomato, peeled, deseeded and diced

Sounds unlikely, I know. But try it. I first made this in France with a French friend in the eighties. And it really is rather an eighties recipe, with both cream and booze in it. But it's definitely worth reviving. You would not believe how so much vinegar cooks down to a mellow sauce with only a little vinegar zing to it.

1. Heat the butter and oil together in a large sauté pan and thoroughly brown the chicken pieces all over, skin side first. Add the garlic and cover the pan. Cook over a low heat for 20 minutes, or until the chicken is tender and cooked through. Remove the chicken (leaving the garlic in the pan) and keep warm in a serving dish. Pour off the fat from the pan.

2. Add the vinegar to the pan, stirring well and scraping up any sediment from the bottom. Boil rapidly until the liquid is reduced to about 2 tablespoons. Add the wine, brandy, mustard and tomato purée, mix well and boil until you have a thick sauce (about 5 minutes at a fast boil).

3. In a small, heavy-based saucepan, boil the cream until reduced by half, stirring frequently to prevent burning. Remove from the heat and set a wire sieve over the pan. Push the vinegar sauce through the sieve, pressing the garlic cloves well to extract their pulp. Scrape the bottom of the sieve with your spoon to include all the sauce. Taste the sauce and season with salt and pepper.

4. Pour the sauce over the chicken and sprinkle with the cashews and diced tomato.

The deliciousness of this dish – and it *is* delicious – depends on the vigorous reduction of the vinegar and wine. If the acids are not properly boiled down, the sauce will be too sharp. Five cloves of garlic seems a lot, but the resulting smooth sauce does not taste particularly strongly of garlic.

John's slow-cooked brisket

Serves 6

cooking oil for frying

1.35kg brisket, boned and rolled

1 x 400g tin chopped tomatoes

1 small can Guinness or other stout

1 tbsp dark brown sugar

2 heaped tbsp tomato purée

1 mild or medium-hot chilli, deseeded and chopped

4 large onions, sliced

2 garlic cloves, crushed

salt and pepper to season

When I first met my husband John, he asked if I'd written a recipe for brisket. Of course, I said, handing him *Leith's Cookery Bible*. He thumbed through the index. No brisket. So here you are, John, eight years late. And you must admit that, as my chief taster, you did declare it worth the calories.

1. Heat the oven to 130°C/fan 110°C/gas mark 1.

2. Very lightly grease the bottom of a large frying pan with oil and brown the brisket well all over. Transfer to a slow cooker, Dutch oven or lidded casserole. Pour off any fat from the frying pan into a cup and add a dollop of the tinned tomatoes to the pan to loosen any brown stuck-on bits with a wooden spoon – you don't want to waste the flavour. Then add the rest of the tomatoes, the stout, sugar, tomato purée and the chilli. Tip over the meat in the casserole.

3. Rinse out the frying pan, then fry the onions in a couple of tablespoons of the fat you kept from browning the meat. Or use cooking oil. Stir frequently to until the onions are even pale brown. Add the garlic and fry for 2 minutes more, then tip on top of the meat.

4. Make sure the lid fits really well (if it doesn't, cover with foil) and cook in the middle of the oven for 4 hours, turning the meat over and stirring the onions and sauce after 2 hours. When the time is up, test with a fork – the meat should be soft and falling into shreds.

5. When done, lift the meat out into a serving dish, spoon off any visible fat from the sauce, check the seasoning and pour over the brisket.

Timing all depends on temperature. Slow-cooking a big piece of meat will take about 4 hours in an oven, as here. On the lowest setting of an electric slow cooker, it could take 6 hours. The coolest oven at the bottom of an Aga might take all day or all night.

Pancake beef pie

10 French pancakes (see recipe on page 230)

500g lean minced beef

cooking oil for frying

3 rashers of rindless streaky bacon, finely diced

1 large onion, finely chopped

1 celery stick, finely chopped

1 garlic clove, crushed

1 x 400g tin chopped tomatoes

1 tbsp tomato purée

a pinch of dried or 1 tsp chopped fresh thyme

salt and pepper to season

To serve

1 tbsp flat-leaf parsley leaves, chopped

190g soured cream or plain yoghurt

(Pictured overleaf.)

I love this recipe. It's not unlike a beef cannelloni or spaghetti bolognese in flavour, but it's more fun to do, looks festive on the table – and each slice, showing the layers of pancake and fillings, makes it look much more difficult to make than it is. It also freezes well and children love it.

1. Following the recipe on page 230, make the pancake batter and allow it to stand while you prepare the meat sauce.

2. Fry half the mince in a hot frying pan with a tablespoon of oil. Press the meat down in a shallow layer on the hot pan with a fish slice, leave while it sizzles and browns, then turn over and fry the other side. This takes a while – the meat needs to be brown all over, not grey. Even if the cooker top ends up messy, it's worth it.

3. Lift the meat out with a slotted spoon and place in a saucepan. 'Deglaze' the frying pan by adding a splash of water and loosening the stuck-bits on the pan bottom with the fish slice. Tip into the saucepan.

4. Repeat with the rest of the mince, transferring it to the saucepan when it's done. Turn the heat down a bit and, using more oil as you need it, fry the bacon, onion, celery and garlic until just turning brown. Then stir in the tomatoes and bring to the boil, still stirring. Pour over the meat in the saucepan and add the tomato purée, thyme and a splash of water. Season with salt and pepper, then simmer gently for 30 minutes, or until thick and syrupy.

5. While the sauce simmers, fry the pancakes. If you are going to eat the pancake pie when ready, keep the pancakes warm in the folds of a tea towel in a low oven. If not, just pile them up.

6. Go back to the meat sauce. If it is too thick, add a little water; if too runny, keep simmering until it is thick and barely liquid. Give it a stir now and then to stop it sticking. Taste and adjust seasoning, if needed.

7. Place a pancake in an ovenproof dish (or on a serving dish, if serving straight away) and spoon over a thin layer of meat sauce. Cover with a second pancake. Continue to layer the meat sauce and pancakes, finishing with a pancake. Spread the sauce evenly to the edge of each pancake, rather than piling it all in the middle.

8. If freezing the pie for later, now is the moment: put it, dish and all, into a freezer bag, leaving the end open to let out the steam until the pie is cold. Then close the bag, chill and freeze. Thaw overnight before reheating, covered with foil, in a warm oven: 40 minutes at 150°C/fan 130°C/gas mark 2.

9. Sprinkle the parsley over the pie and serve with cream or yoghurt on the side.

Ultimate cottage pie
with black pudding

Serves 4

cooking oil for frying

500g lean minced beef

100g black pudding

3 rashers of rindless streaky bacon, diced

1 large onion, finely chopped

1 celery stick, finely chopped

1 garlic clove, crushed

1 x 400g tin chopped tomatoes

1 tbsp tomato purée

a pinch of dried or 1 tsp chopped fresh thyme

salt and pepper to season

For the mash

250g Maris Piper potatoes, cut into 5–6cm (2in) chunks

500g sweet potatoes, cut into 5–6cm (2in) chunks

about 50g butter

2 tbsp grated strong Cheddar cheese

1 tbsp fresh breadcrumbs

Cottage pie can be a sorry affair: grey, wet mince under watery mash, neither with much flavour. Or it can be sublime: rich, dark mince with creamy mash and a crusty, cheesy top. It's all in the frying, so follow the instructions below and never mind if the cooker top ends up a mess.

1. Heat a tablespoon of oil in a heavy-based frying pan. If the mince is in a lump, flatten it on a plate. If it is in a supermarket pack, keep it flat. Press the slab of mince into the really hot pan using a fish slice, and leave it there, without fiddling with it, for 2 minutes or more, then sneak a look to see if it's really brown. Flip it over and repeat. When both sides are brown, break it up to brown all the meat. Lift out with a slotted spoon and drop into a saucepan. Cook the black pudding as you have the mince, then remove with a slotted spoon and add to the saucepan.

2. 'Deglaze' the frying pan by adding a splash of water and loosening the stuck-on bits with the fish slice. Tip onto the cooked meat. Turn down the heat under the pan and, using more oil as needed, fry the bacon, onion, celery and garlic until just turning brown. Stir in the tomatoes and bring to the boil, still stirring, then pour into the pan with the meat and black pudding. Add the tomato purée and thyme, and season. Simmer gently for 45 minutes, or until the sauce is thick and syrupy.

3. If the sauce is too thick, add a little water; if too runny, simmer until it is thick and barely liquid, stirring now and then to stop it sticking. Season well, then spoon into a pie dish deep enough for the mixture to reach 2–3cm (1in) from the top. Smooth the top, then allow to cool a bit and form a skin.

4. Heat the oven to 180°C/fan 160°C/gas mark 4 and start on the mash. Boil the potatoes and the sweet potatoes in separate saucepans of lightly salted water for 15–25 minutes until tender enough to mash. Drain well and return to the pans. Add one or two thick slices of butter to each and mash well with a hand masher or stick blender, until light and smooth. Combine the two purées and season with salt and pepper.

5. Top the mince with spoonfuls of the mash, starting around the edges, until covered. Gently press down with the back of a fork. Mix the cheese and crumbs together and sprinkle on top of the pie. Bake for 25 minutes if the meat and mash are still hot, 45–50 minutes if they are cold.

Bobotie

Serves 6

2 thick slices of white bread

150ml milk

3 tbsp vegetable oil

2 large onions, finely chopped

2 garlic cloves, crushed

3cm (1in) piece of ginger, peeled and finely grated

1 tbsp mild curry powder

1 tsp ground coriander

½ tsp ground cumin

450g lamb mince

1 small dessert apple, grated

75g fruit chutney

2 tbsp Worcestershire sauce

1 tbsp tomato purée

a handful of sultanas

salt and pepper to season

For the custard

2 medium eggs

275g Greek yoghurt

a handful of flaked almonds

2 kaffir lime leaves or bay leaves (see Tip)

I'm South African by birth, and the one dish I remember loving all through my childhood is this. It's a sort of cross between a shepherd's pie and moussaka, mildly curried, and is a reflection of South Africa's history of Dutch and Malaysian influences. It is great for a party – unusual enough to surprise people, but not so exotic as to put off the children. It will sit in a warm oven for hours.

1. Put the bread into a small tray or shallow bowl and pour over the milk. Leave to soak. Heat the oven to 180°C/fan 160°C/gas mark 4.

2. Heat half the oil in a large, heavy-based saucepan over a medium-high heat. Add the onions and fry until soft and just golden. Add the garlic, ginger, curry powder, coriander and cumin and cook for a further minute or so. Transfer into a large bowl.

3. Wipe the saucepan clean and pour in the remaining oil. Turn the heat up and fry the lamb mince for 5–6 minutes, until golden brown. Press the meat down with a fish slice to encourage it to brown properly. When the meat is browned on all sides, add it to the spiced onions, along with the apple, chutney, Worcestershire sauce, tomato purée and sultanas. Add a little water if it looks too thick. Fork the wet bread into the mixture, season and gently combine. Pile the mixture into a 2-litre ovenproof dish and use the back of a wooden spoon to flatten it.

4. Mix the eggs with the yoghurt. Season with salt and pepper, then pour over the mixture. Scatter with the almonds, then place the kaffir leaves on top and bake for about 40–45 minutes, until the custard topping has set and browned. Remove the bobotie from the oven and let it stand for 10 minutes before serving.

> This is the traditional way to make bobotie, but when we were little this was often made from leftover roast lamb. Don't fry the meat, just chop or mince it finely, then mix with the spiced onions.
>
> Bobotie is always topped with a couple of leaves. In South Africa the dish is generally topped with kaffir lime leaves; in England they are usually bay leaves.

Smoked haddock
and spinach filo parcels

Makes 4

a little olive oil

150g baby spinach leaves

3 spring onions, finely chopped

40g flaked almonds

1 small egg, beaten

75g cream cheese

75g feta, crumbled

600g smoked haddock fillets, skinned

6 sheets filo pastry

50g butter, melted

salt and pepper to season

Lots of cooks are nervous about cooking fish, which is odd since there are only two golden rules: the fresher the fish, the better; and don't overcook it. This dish is a good one for a beginner. It's simple and delicious. You can be as neat as you like, but I rather like filo to look crumpled and casual.

1. Heat the oven to 200°C/fan 180°C/gas mark 6.

2. Heat the olive oil in a large frying pan over a medium-high heat. Drop the spinach into the pan, tossing the leaves just until they have wilted. Gather them into a clump and transfer to a sieve, draining any excess water by pressing with kitchen paper. You want the spinach to be fairly dry. Chop roughly.

3. Mix the spring onions, flaked almonds, egg, cream cheese, feta and chopped spinach in a bowl and combine well. Season with black pepper and possibly a little salt (the feta will already be salty, so be careful).

4. Divide the fish into four. It doesn't matter if each portion is one large piece or a couple of smaller ones.

5. Keeping any filo you are not working with tightly covered with cling film to prevent it from drying out, paint a sheet of filo with melted butter, then fold it in half and butter it again. Put one portion of the haddock in the middle and spoon a quarter of the spinach mixture on top. Bring the corners of the filo up over the fish, then use a half-sheet of buttered filo and wrap the parcel again, squashing the filo roughly around the fish and pinching it together at the top. Repeat to make three more parcels. Don't worry if they look a bit rough; they'll look great when hot and brown.

6. Put the parcels on a greased baking sheet or on a tray covered with baking parchment and bake for 20 minutes until lightly coloured.

> Filo sheets come in different sizes, so you may need to cut them to fit. The thing is to wrap the parcels first in two layers of filo, then more loosely in a single sheet.
>
> You can also make filo parcels with salmon and tarragon, mackerel and ready-cooked lentils, goat's cheese and slices of red pepper …

Rib-eye steak with chips

(Pictured overleaf.)

Serves 4

4 x 220g sirloin steaks

olive oil for frying

salt and pepper to season

For the chips

800g Maris Piper potatoes

600ml vegetable oil

1 tsp sea salt

1 tsp mild curry powder

For the herb butter

2 tbsp flat-leaf parsley
leaves, chopped

1 tbsp tarragon leaves,
chopped

1 tbsp chives, chopped

1 tbsp mint leaves, chopped

1 tsp Dijon mustard

80g butter, softened

salt and pepper to season

The perfect rib-eye steak is surprisingly easy to achieve. But you need really good meat, blazing heat and the confidence to know when it's done. Grass-fed, well-aged beef from a named farm and a named breed, say Aberdeen Angus or Dexter, is going to be expensive; but all grilling steak is pricey, and I'd rather have something exceptional once in a blue moon than a tasteless or tough steak more often.

The blazing heat could be a barbecue, grill or frying pan, the easiest of which is probably the pan. You just have to be prepared for a bit of splattering: trust me, it's worth it. And who can resist fresh-from-the-fryer chips? I like them any way at all: classic French fries, matchstick thin, potato skins, fried in beef dripping or goose fat. But most of all I like them as big, fat, rectangular blocks, twice-fried, skin on, then dusted with curry powder and salt. That's how we served them at The Hoxton Apprentice, a charity restaurant I helped set up to train disadvantaged young people to be cooks. We ate rather more of them than the customers!

1. Remove the steak from the fridge about half an hour before cooking to allow it to come to room temperature.

2. Leaving the skin on, cut the potatoes into chunky, stubby 2.5cm (1in) chips. Pour the vegetable oil into a large, heavy-based saucepan – it should reach about 5cm (2in) deep – and place over a high heat. If you own a cooking thermometer, bring the temperature of the oil to about 130°C; if not, add a raw chip or cube of bread to the oil – when it starts to float and fry, the oil is hot enough.

3. Use a large metal spoon or sieve to gently lower the chips into the hot oil and fry for about 5 minutes, until they are tender when poked with a skewer but not browned. For this first frying (the chips are going in twice), the oil should bubble, but not too vigorously. Drain the chips on kitchen paper and set aside until completely cold.

4. Make the herb butter by mashing all the ingredients together. Form into a sausage shape, wrap in cling film and chill in the fridge.

5. Heat a large, heavy frying pan or griddle over a high heat. Rub each steak with olive oil and season generously on both sides. Once the pan

is really hot, add two of the steaks. For medium-rare, cook the steaks for about 3 minutes without moving them, then turn them over. You can tell when they are ready to turn, because the heat under them will have forced the juices to the surface and the top of the steak will look moist and shiny. At that stage they should be browned. Give them 2 minutes or so on the other side, then remove from the pan and allow to rest on a warm plate loosely covered with foil and a clean tea towel. Cook the other steaks and leave them all to rest while you finish the chips.

6. Heat the oil again, this time to 135°C. If necessary, cook the chips in two batches so as not to lower the oil temperature too much. Lower the once-cooked chips into the oil using a metal spoon or sieve and fry for approximately 5 minutes until golden brown. Lift them from the fryer and drop into a bowl lined with kitchen paper. Shake them around a little before removing the paper and gently tossing the chips in curry powder and salt. Mix to combine.

7. Just before serving, top each steak with a slice of herb butter. Serve the chips in the middle of the table for diners to help themselves (or try to resist temptation!)

Here's how to tell how rare a steak is. It's done by pressing it with a finger. First, teach yourself how blue, rare, medium or well-done steak feels with this neat trick. Hold your left-hand palm upward and lightly touch your thumb and first finger together. Don't press. With a finger of your right hand feel the fleshy pad at the bottom of your left thumb. It feels squashy and soft, doesn't it? Right, that's what blue steak feels like. Now touch your thumb to the end of your middle finger (lightly remember, don't press). That's what rare steak feels like. Now put thumb and ring finger together – that's medium. Finally touch your thumb to your pinkie: that's well done. Basically, the more cooked it is, the firmer the steak will feel.

It is worth making herb butter in quantity. I generally make several little rolls of it, slice them into 1cm (½ in) rounds and freeze them. Then, when I want one for a chop, steak, fish fillet or seafood, or just to spread on bread, I don't have to chop tiny amounts of herbs.

Puds

Rum Nicky with clotted cream

Serves 4–6

For the filling

225g dates, stoned and coarsely chopped

100g dried apricots, coarsely chopped

50g stem ginger in syrup, drained and finely chopped

50ml dark rum

50g soft dark brown sugar

50g unsalted butter, cut into 1–2cm (½ in) cubes

For the shortcrust pastry

200g plain flour

100g unsalted butter, chilled and cut into small cubes

1 medium egg, beaten

a squeeze of lemon juice

1 medium egg yolk, beaten, for brushing

To serve

clotted cream

I'd never heard of this until I found myself on *Bake Off* with Paul Hollywood. The recipe originates from his home town of Liverpool. There are two theories about the name. One was that the dockers unloading the ships from the Caribbean would 'nick' a bit of rum, which their wives would use to make the pies. Or, more boringly, that the name came from the nicks made in the pastry lid to let the steam escape. I tested the recipe like this, but decided a lattice top was better.

The pie is best made in an old-fashioned enamel pie-plate, which allows the bottom crust to cook through much better than a ceramic one.

1. Mix all the filling ingredients, except the butter, together in a bowl. Set aside.

2. For the pastry, put the flour, butter, egg, lemon juice and 2 tablespoons of cold water into a food processor and whizz to a ball. (If making by hand, rub the butter lightly into the flour until it resembles breadcrumbs. Mix the egg with the lemon juice and water and add to the flour mixture. Using a table knife, work the liquid into the flour and bring the pastry together. Use your hands to gently knead it into a ball.) Wrap the dough in cling film and rest in the fridge for at least 15 minutes.

3. Heat the oven to 180°C/fan 160°C/gas mark 4, and put a baking sheet on the middle shelf to heat.

4. Cut a third off the ball of dough and set aside. Roll out the rest of the dough on a floured work surface into a circle large enough to line a 20cm (8in) enamel pie-plate. Transfer to the pie-plate, easing it into the corners. Spread out the filling in the pastry case and dot with the butter. Flatten the top.

5. Roll out the remaining pastry and cut it into 1cm (½ in) wide strips. Lay four or five of the strips parallel across the filling to cover the pie. Lay another four or five strips across the first lot, not directly at right angles but at a slight slant to give diamond-shaped gaps. Trim the ends of each strip neatly and tuck them between the filling and pastry rim. Trim the edges with a sharp knife, then brush the pastry with beaten egg yolk.

6. Bake for 15 minutes, then turn the oven down to 160°C/fan 140°C/ gas mark 3 and cook for a further 20 minutes. Serve with clotted cream.

Plum clafoutis

Serves 4–6

For the pudding

1 tsp vanilla extract

150ml milk

100ml double cream

4 medium eggs

100g caster sugar

30g plain flour

a pinch of salt

20g butter

1 tbsp soft brown sugar

6 large plums or
400g damsons

1½ tsp ground allspice

To serve

icing sugar

single cream (optional)

I ate my first clafoutis in France, when I was working as an au pair in the sixties. It was made with damsons we'd picked off the tree growing behind the village church. I still think damsons make the best clafoutis. Now, as a septuagenarian, I'm lucky enough to have a damson tree in my garden. Every year it gives me buckets and buckets of fruit. Why doesn't anyone sell them commercially? It's crazy.

If you can make a Yorkshire pud, you can make this heavenly plum pud. If you can get hold of damsons, so much the better, but cherries, greengages, peaches and apricots are all delicious too.

1. Heat the oven to 180°C/fan 160°C/gas mark 4.

2. Blend the vanilla, milk, double cream, eggs, caster sugar, flour and salt together in a liquidizer, then leave for the flour to swell in the liquid for 20 minutes or so.

3. Meanwhile, spread the butter in a wide, shallow 1.25-litre baking dish. Sprinkle in the brown sugar.

4. Halve and stone the plums or damsons and spread out evenly in the dish. Dust the allspice over them, then roast for 10 minutes.

5. Remove from the oven and immediately pour over the batter. Bake in the middle of the oven for 35 minutes. The clafoutis should be risen and brown. Dust with icing sugar and serve at once, with cream if liked.

For an amazing clafoutis, add a good glug of brandy to the plums before baking. Or, instead of fresh fruit, use a jar of cherries marinated in kirsch, or ready-to-eat dried apricots with a slug of amaretto liqueur.

Hot apricot and blood orange soufflé

120g dried apricots, soaked for 2 hours in 200ml water

20g butter plus extra for greasing

20g plain flour

100ml blood orange juice

finely grated zest of 1 blood orange

3 medium egg whites

30g caster sugar

icing sugar, for dusting

Orange Baci di Dama with Rosemary biscuits to serve (see opposite)

(Pictured overleaf.)

This is a feather-light, modern take on the rich old-fashioned cream-and-egg-laden soufflé. It is just as delicious, but contains no cream.

1. Heat the oven to 200°C/fan 180°C/gas mark 6 and put a baking sheet on the middle shelf to heat.

2. Tip the soaked apricots and their soaking water into a saucepan and poach, covered, over a low heat until tender; about 20 minutes. Spoon out the apricots and put into a liquidizer with 1 tablespoon of their poaching liquor. Blend until smooth.

3. Lightly grease four 200ml or six 150ml ramekins with butter and dust with caster sugar.

4. Melt the butter in a small saucepan, add the flour and cook for 1 minute. Remove from the heat and add the orange juice and zest. Mix well before adding the apricot purée. Return to a medium heat and simmer for 2–3 minutes, stirring constantly. Remove from the heat and allow to cool.

5. In a large bowl, whisk the egg whites until they will hold their shape. Add the sugar and whisk again until stiff.

6. Tip all the apricot mix into the egg-white bowl. Gently fold the two mixtures together, then spoon into the ramekins, filling them almost to the top.

7. Run your finger around the inside top edge of each ramekin to get a 'top hat' appearance to the cooked soufflés. Bake in the oven, on the hot baking sheet, for 12–14 minutes. Test by giving one of the ramekins a slight shake. If the soufflé wobbles alarmingly, it needs further cooking. If it wobbles only slightly, it's ready. Dust with icing sugar and serve immediately with the Baci di Dama biscuits.

If you don't want to fiddle with individual little soufflés, make one big soufflé in a 15cm (6in) soufflé dish – it will take about 25 minutes to cook.

Orange baci di dama
with rosemary

Makes 20

100g butter, softened

100g caster sugar

100g ground almonds

100g plain flour

finely grated zest of 1 orange

½ tbsp finely chopped
rosemary

20 apricot kernels
(see Tip below) or
10 almonds, halved

(Pictured overleaf.)

These melt-in-the-mouth 'ladies' kisses' are irresistible. They can be made with other flavours, but I think orange and rosemary is a great combination.

1. Heat the oven to 180°C/fan 160°C/gas mark 4.

2. Beat the butter and sugar together until smooth and light, either by hand or machine. Add the ground almonds, flour, orange zest and rosemary and work the mixture until it forms a stiff dough.

3. Shape into twenty small balls, then arrange on baking sheets, leaving a 3–4cm (1½ in) gap in between each one. Press an apricot kernel or almond in the centre of each ball and bake for 10 minutes. Cool on a wire rack.

These are delicious served with coffee or ice cream too, anywhere you can ration them to one or two per person. Put them in a biscuit tin and they'll be gone by morning.

Apricot kernels – like tiny, powerfully fragrant almonds – can be bought online, but they are much cheaper from an organic food shop. Please note that The Food Standards Agency advise us not to eat too many of them as they can be toxic – another good reason to avoid eating more than a couple of these biscuits at a time!

Amaretti and lemon curd trifle

Serves 8

175g amaretti biscuits

100ml sherry

500ml fresh vanilla custard

250g fresh raspberries

300ml double cream

200ml lemon curd

2–3 tbsp pistachios, chopped (see Tip below)

1 tbsp freeze-dried raspberries

There's nothing like an English trifle, but there's not always time to make one from scratch. This recipe is simplicity itself, using good-quality ready-made vanilla custard.

This is a great family favourite. I can't stand jelly in trifle because for some reason I hate the feel of bits of cake spoiling smooth silky jelly. It's like biscuit crumbs in the bed. Besides, the combination of creamy custard, good jam and cake is perfection. Go mad with the topping – I use anything and everything I can find in the store cupboard.

1. Scrunch 100g of the amaretti biscuits into chunky bits and empty into a trifle dish. Sprinkle over two-thirds of the sherry. Dollop over the custard, completely covering the biscuits. Scatter the fresh raspberries over the custard, making sure some sit towards the sides of the bowl so they're visible.

2. Next up is a second layer of scrunched biscuits and the final soaking of sherry. Pause at this point and chill the trifle for a few hours or overnight.

3. Whip the cream to soft, gentle peaks and fold almost all the lemon curd into it – keeping back about 1 tablespoon for decoration. Do not over-mix; it's lovely to see streaks of curd in the cream. Spoon on top of the trifle, then finish with a final swirl of lemon curd and a sprinkling of pistachios and freeze-dried raspberries.

Try to buy beautiful pistachio nibs from a Lebanese shop. They show off the stunning green colour, so are well worth the trouble of sourcing. Alternatively, rub off the papery skins of the pistachios and discard. Finely chop the nuts with a sharp knife (a machine seems to grind them down so that the nut dust dulls the vivid green).

Peggy's passion-fruit cream

Serves 4

300ml double cream

100ml Cointreau or Van Der Hum

seeds and flesh from 8 passion fruit

(Pictured overleaf.)

My mother, Peggy, was a rotten cook, but this little number, requiring no time at all and no skill, turned up a lot, mostly for summer parties. I still make it.

1. Whip the cream until it will just hold its shape. Stir in the liqueur. Layer it up in glasses with the passion fruit.

Muscovado heaven

Serves 4

150ml double cream

150g plain yoghurt

about 3 tbsp dark muscovado sugar

(Pictured overleaf.)

This is a dish I thought I'd invented – until I saw Nigella had an almost identical recipe called Barbados Dream. Ah well! Make sure you buy dark muscovado sugar – it's the only sugar that gives that dark treacly taste and aroma. You'll find it in big supermarkets or health food stores. This is a popular quick pud in our house.

1. Lightly whip the cream. Mix with the yoghurt and spoon the mixture into four individual glasses.

2. Sprinkle generously with muscovado sugar and chill in the fridge for half an hour or so. The sugar will dissolve into a dark lake and, with luck, will run attractively down the inside of the glasses. If you like a bit of crunch, sprinkle a little more sugar on top before serving.

Stewed fruit or compote works with this. Many types of fresh fruit, such as raspberries, go watery, but try mango, blueberries or banana.

Muscavodo sugar goes as hard as concrete if it dries out. I keep mine in a sealed plastic canister, but even this is not entirely airtight. I follow a tip from my Granny Leith in South Africa: put half an apple, cut-side down, on the sugar in the tin. The sugar preserves the apple and the apple keeps the sugar moist and soft. After a few months the apple will shrink and dry out but it won't go mouldy.

Summer berry compote on vanilla ice cream

Serves 6

Vanilla Ice Cream
(see page 241)

For the compote

500g summer berries
(raspberries, blackberries,
strawberries, blueberries,
blackcurrants)

50g caster sugar

½ tsp grated nutmeg
(optional)

3 cardamom pods, bashed
(optional)

3cm (1in) piece of ginger,
sliced into 3 (optional)

Chocolate and Macadamia
Biscotti to serve
(see page 255)

(Pictured overleaf.)

This is wonderful on top of vanilla ice cream. I first ate it fifty years ago at the Vienna Opera House in the interval, and I'm ashamed to say I've forgotten the opera but still remember the ice cream. I serve the compote cold in the summer and warm and spicy in the winter. I make it when there's a glut of berries in the garden or when they can be had cheaply, making some plain and some spiced. The biscotti turn what could be a breakfast dish into a dessert posh enough for a dinner party.

1. In a saucepan, simmer the fruit with 50ml water and the sugar for 4–5 minutes, just until the berries begin to burst. Strain through a nylon sieve set over a bowl and allow to drip for 5 minutes or so.

2. Return the juice to the saucepan, reserving the berries for later. (For the spiced version, add the nutmeg, cardamom and ginger now). Simmer for about 6–8 minutes over a medium heat, until thick, syrupy and reduced by half. Strain out the flavourings, if any, and add the berries. Allow to cool, then chill in the fridge.

3. Put a ball or two of ice cream into each glass and top with the chilled compote. Or serve the ice cream in bowls and hand round the compote separately. Serve with the biscotti.

Greek yoghurt with rose-petal jam and pistachio

Serves 4

400g Greek yoghurt

4 tbsp rose-petal jam

50g pistachios, chopped

dried or crystallized rose
petals

(Pictured overleaf.)

Jocelyn Dimbleby, a great traveller, introduced me to Turkish rose-petal jam. You can buy it (and dried petals) in Turkish or Lebanese shops or online. To crystallize rose petals, brush dark red petals with unbeaten egg white, dust with caster sugar and leave in a warm place to dry.

1. Layer up the yoghurt and jam in glasses and top with the nuts and rose petals.

Ultimate French pancakes

110g plain flour

a pinch of salt

1 medium egg

1 medium egg yolk

290ml whole milk, or milk
and water mixed

1 tbsp sunflower oil

oil or butter for frying

lemon wedges and caster
sugar to serve

A good French pancake should be too thin to toss with ease. When I was at cookery school, our teacher used to say that if we could toss it we should toss it out!

1. Put all the ingredients except the fat for frying in a liquidizer or food processor and whizz briefly. (In the absence of a machine, sift the flour with the salt into a bowl and make a well in the centre, exposing the bottom of the bowl. Put the egg and egg yolk, along with a little of the milk, into this well. Using a fork or whisk, mix the egg and milk together, at first without drawing in the surrounding flour. When smooth, gradually draw in the flour from the sides as you mix. When the mixture reaches the consistency of thick cream, beat well and stir in the sunflower oil. Add the remaining milk; the consistency should now be that of single cream.) Leave the batter to rest for 30 minutes.

2. Lightly grease a 23cm (9in) frying pan with oil or butter, wiping out any excess with kitchen paper, and put over a medium-low heat. Pour about a tablespoon of batter into the pan and swirl until it's evenly spread across the bottom. Cook until set, then, using a palette knife and your fingers, turn the pancake over (it should be pale brown) and cook on the other side. The pancakes should be extremely thin, so if the first one is too thick, add a little extra milk to the batter. The first pancake is unlikely to be perfect, and is often discarded.

3. Use the remaining batter to make more pancakes, turning them out onto a clean tea towel or plate. Serve with lemon wedges and a dusting of caster sugar.

Apple caramel cake

Serves 16

125g medjool dates, stoned and finely chopped

5 tbsp cloudy apple juice

325g unsalted butter, softened

250g light brown muscovado sugar

5 medium eggs, at room temperature, beaten

300g self-raising flour

¼ tsp baking powder

2 tbsp ground cinnamon

2 tsp ground mixed spice

60g dried apple rings or slices, finely chopped

For the buttercream

175g golden caster sugar

175ml double cream

175g unsalted butter, softened

100g icing sugar, sifted

125g full-fat cream cheese

1–1½ tsp vanilla extract

For the toffee apples

1 Bramley apple

85g golden caster sugar

(Pictured overleaf.)

This is quite a cake! I adapted this recipe from one by Steven Carter-Bailey, who was a *Bake Off* finalist in 2017. The sponge layers are made with dates, spices and pieces of dried apple, and are then sandwiched together with a caramel buttercream.

It is a huge celebratory affair, but it need not be this big. Just halve the quantities and cook in two tins for 5 minutes less (the mixture will not be so deep). And, of course, if you don't have time to fiddle about making mini toffee apples, just leave them out.

1. Start by making the date purée: put the dates and the apple juice into a small pan and cook gently over a low heat, stirring frequently, for about 10 minutes, until thick and soft. Remove the pan from the heat and mash the contents to make a coarse, thick purée. Leave to cool.

2. Heat the oven to 180°C/fan 160°C/gas mark 4. Grease three 20cm (8in) round, deep sandwich tins and line with baking parchment.

3. Put the butter into a large bowl, or the bowl of a mixer, and beat for 2 minutes until very light. Scrape down the sides of the bowl, then add the brown sugar and beat thoroughly for 5 minutes until light and fluffy.

4. Gradually add the eggs, beating well after each addition. Sift the flour, baking powder, cinnamon and mixed spice into the bowl and fold in gently. Add the cooled date purée and the dried apple. The mixture should drop easily from a tapped spoon/spatula – if it seems a bit stiff, stir in an extra tablespoon or so of apple juice.

5. Divide the mixture equally between the three tins and spread evenly with a palette knife or spoon. Bake the sponges for about 20–22 minutes, until risen, golden brown and springy. Cool for 5 minutes before carefully turning out onto a wire rack. Leave to cool completely.

6. For the buttercream, start with the caramel sauce base: put the sugar and 3 tablespoons of water into a heavy-based medium saucepan (not non-stick, as you need to see the colour of the caramel) and set over a low heat to melt very gently. Stir occasionally, and keep a bowl of water and a heatproof pastry brush handy, so you can brush down the sides of the pan to dislodge any sugar crystals. Meanwhile, gently warm the cream.

7. Once the sugar has completely dissolved, turn up the heat and boil rapidly, without stirring, until the syrup turns a rich caramel brown. Remove the pan from the heat, cover your hand with an oven glove (the mixture will splutter and foam up and may burn you if it touches your skin) and slowly pour in the warmed cream. Return the pan to a low heat and whisk with a hand whisk for about a minute, until the sauce is very smooth and thick. Pour into a heatproof bowl, leave to cool, then cover and chill for about 1 hour or until firm.

8. Beat the butter for a couple of minutes until very light. Add the icing sugar and mix (starting on a slow speed to avoid a mess) for 5 minutes, until very light and fluffy. Scrape down the sides of the bowl and beat in the cream cheese, followed by the cold caramel sauce and the vanilla extract. When thoroughly combined, cover and (if necessary) chill until firm enough to spread easily.

10. To assemble the cake: set one sponge, top-side down, on a serving plate. Divide the buttercream in half and set aside one half for topping and decorating the cake. Spread the sponge with half the remaining buttercream, then top with another sponge, pressing it lightly in place. Repeat the process with the other half of the buttercream. Cover with the third sponge, top-side up, and gently press the whole cake so it is firm and level.

11. Coat the sides of the cake thinly with the reserved buttercream to give a 'naked cake' appearance, then spread the remaining buttercream on the top, swirling it attractively. Leave to firm up overnight somewhere cool.

12. The following day, make the mini toffee apples. Lightly oil a large baking sheet or piece of baking parchment. Peel the apple, leaving it whole. Use a melon baller to scoop out round balls from the apple flesh, avoiding the core. Pat dry and leave on kitchen paper while you make the caramel.

13. Put the sugar and 3 tablespoons of water into a small saucepan, dissolve gently, then boil until you have a rich caramel. Remove the pan from the heat and, using a cocktail stick to spear each apple ball, dip it into the caramel to coat. Lift out and twirl around for a few seconds until it has stopped dripping. Then ease the ball off the cocktail stick onto the oiled surface and leave to cool. Keep the balls well separated, as they will stick together given half a chance.

14. When you are ready to serve, decorate the cake with the sticky toffee apples and serve.

Devil's food cake

Serves 12–16

This is simply the best chocolate cake I've ever eaten. It was given to me by Rebecca, who works behind the scenes for *Bake Off*. She is a brilliant baker. She says the recipe is her mum's. So thank you, Rebecca's mum. It's so lovely that recipes get passed along, spreading joy to the world.

For the chocolate frosting

200ml double cream

350g butter

450g dark chocolate, finely chopped

For the sponges

75g cocoa powder, sifted

150g light brown sugar

2 tsp vanilla paste

335g plain flour

1 tsp baking powder

1 tsp bicarbonate of soda

200g butter plus extra for greasing

225g caster sugar

3 large eggs

For the decoration

150g dark chocolate (70% cocoa solids)

1. For the chocolate frosting, pour the cream into a saucepan, add the butter and heat, stirring occasionally, until the butter has melted. Bring to just below boiling point, then remove from the heat. Add the chocolate and whisk until smooth and glossy. Pour into a bowl and leave to set at room temperature, whisking occasionally.

2. Heat the oven to 180°C/fan 160°C/gas mark 4 and grease and line three 20cm (8in) loose-bottomed sandwich tins with baking parchment.

3. For the sponges, put the cocoa powder, light brown sugar, vanilla paste and 375ml boiling water in a bowl and whisk together until the sugar has dissolved. Set aside. Sieve the flour, baking powder and bicarbonate of soda together into another bowl.

4. Cream the butter and caster sugar together in a separate bowl until pale and fluffy, then beat in the eggs, one at a time, mixing in a tablespoon of the flour mix after each egg. Add the rest of the flour, a third at a time, folding well to disperse any flour pockets.

5. Fold in the cooled cocoa mixture, then divide between the three tins and bake for 25–30 minutes, until risen and a skewer inserted into the centre comes out clean.

6. Remove from the oven, leave to cool in the tins for 5 minutes, then turn out onto wire racks to cool.

7. For the decoration, melt the chocolate in a bowl set over a pan of gently simmering water. Meanwhile, grease the underside of a baking tray with oil and pour the melted chocolate onto it. Leave to set, then drag a cheese plane over the surface to create curls. Keep these cool.

8. Place a cooled sponge on a cake stand and spread with about a quarter of the frosting. Place another sponge on top and spread with another quarter of the frosting. Place the remaining sponge on top, then spread the remaining frosting over the top and sides of the cake, swirling with a palette knife. Arrange the chocolate curls on top of the cake.

Super-star bananas on toast

Serves 2

For the caramel

130g granulated sugar

20g butter

6 tbsp double cream

1 vanilla pod, split and
seeds scraped

1 tbsp rum

a pinch of salt

1 tbsp brandy

To assemble

a handful of hazelnuts,
peeled and roughly chopped
(see Tip below)

butter for frying

2 small bananas, split
lengthways

2 thick slices of brioche

Vanilla Ice Cream to serve
(see page 241)

This is probably the naughtiest dish in this book. But it's also unbelievably good and for a once-in-a-blue-moon treat, it's worth every calorie.

1. For the caramel, place the sugar and 6 tablespoons of water in a medium-sized saucepan and allow to dissolve over a medium heat. Do not stir the caramel, but swirl the pan gently. Once the sugar has dissolved, boil rapidly until the caramel is a rich golden brown. Remove from the heat and stir in the butter. Add the cream (it will hiss!), vanilla seeds, rum and salt. Allow the caramel to cool a little, then add the brandy. Keep warm.

2. Toast the hazelnuts in a dry frying pan over a medium heat, shaking the pan to brown them all over. Tip out onto a saucer.

3. Add a good knob of butter to the frying pan and lay in the bananas, cut side down. Fry for 2–3 minutes before turning over and cooking the other side. Remove from the heat but keep warm.

4. Toast the brioche slices to a good brown and set each one on a plate. Briefly shake the pan of bananas over the heat to make sure they are hot and arrange them on the toast, pouring over any butter from the pan too. Sprinkle with the toasted hazelnuts, spoon over the warm caramel sauce and add a generous ball of ice cream.

You can toast the hazelnuts and make the caramel sauce ahead, then warm it gently before serving. But the toast and bananas are best done just before you assemble each plate and add the ice cream.

To get the brown, papery skin off hazelnuts, roast them in a hot oven until beginning to brown, then rub them in a clean tea towel.

Mango ice cream

(Pictured overleaf.)

Husband John has a built-in gelato-radar. He can sniff out an ice-cream stall in any town in the world. He's even had mare's milk ice cream in Mongolia. But mango is his favourite, and I'm glad to say he thinks (or at least is wise enough to say) that mine is the best.

Makes 1.2 litres

250ml double cream

1 x 850g tin mango purée

200ml sweetened condensed milk

juice of 2 lemons

1. Whip the double cream to soft peaks and mix with the remaining ingredients. Then you can just freeze it, and thaw when needed. But if you want a lighter texture, freeze the ice cream in a shallow tray and, when frozen, tip out onto a board. Allow to thaw until it's possible to cut into chunks. Blitz the chunks in a food processor until smooth and creamy, then serve, or put back in the freezer to refreeze.

> You can buy tins of mango purée very cheaply online. I like the Kesar brand, which has terrific flavour and very little added sugar.
>
> When you taste the unfrozen mix for any ice cream, remember to make it a little more highly flavoured and sweeter than seems right. When your taste buds are cold – as with a mouthful of ice cream – they shrink and don't work so well, so you need to up the taste.

Basil ice cream

(Pictured overleaf.)

This is dead easy to do – no need for churning.

Makes 1.6 litres

a large bunch of basil (about 100g)

500g caster sugar

250g mascarpone cheese

1kg full-fat plain yoghurt

1. Pick the basil leaves from the stems and put them, along with the sugar, in a food processor. Blitz until combined to a smooth, bright green paste and then blend with the mascarpone and yoghurt. Pour into shallow trays and freeze for an hour until half-frozen. Remove from the freezer and whisk up with a fork. Return to the freezer until completely frozen.

> To soften the ice cream enough to scoop it, take it out of the freezer 15 minutes beforehand, or give it a 30-second blast in the microwave.

Vanilla ice cream

Makes 1 litre

400ml whole milk

400ml double cream

2 vanilla pods

8 medium egg yolks

150g caster sugar

a pinch of salt

(Pictured overleaf.)

You can, of course, buy excellent ready-made ice cream. My fellow judge on *Bake Off* sells his truly delicious Paul Hollywood ones. But sometimes I like to make my own. This one is heaven with the Super-Star Bananas on Toast on the previous page.

1. Put the milk and cream into a large saucepan. Split the vanilla pod in half lengthways and add it to the pan. Bring to a simmer then remove from the heat and set aside for 20 minutes to allow the vanilla flavour to infuse the milk and cream.

2. Whisk the egg yolks with the sugar and salt and then stir in the milk and cream mix and cook over a medium heat, stirring constantly, until the custard coats the back of a wooden spoon. Don't be impatient and turn up the heat – the custard will curdle if it boils. Once thickened to the consistency of single cream, remove from the heat, and fish out the vanilla pod – but don't discard it yet. Strain the custard into a bowl. Scrape the vanilla seeds out of the pod and add them to the custard too. Leave to cool to room temperature.

3. When cool, churn the mixture in an ice-cream machine, then transfer to a plastic container and put into the freezer until needed. Alternatively, freeze the mixture in a shallow tray. When frozen, cut into chunks and briefly whizz it in a food processor, then immediately return to the freezer.

4. Transfer the ice cream from the freezer to the fridge 20–30 minutes before serving, to soften it slightly.

> If you don't have a food processor or an ice-cream maker, all is not lost. Freeze the mixture in a shallow container and, when it's half-frozen, stir it up with a fork, then return to the freezer. Repeat this, whisking up one more time when the ice cream is half-frozen again, and then freeze for the final time.

Ginger ice cream

85g granulated sugar

4 medium egg yolks

2 tsp ground ginger

4 pieces of stem ginger, cut into fine strips

600ml double cream

Vanilla Ice-box Biscuits to serve (see opposite)

(Pictured overleaf.)

I love ginger in anything, but especially in ice cream. Make sure you chop the stem ginger really finely and give the mix a blitz or fork-up once it is half-frozen, so that the pieces will be evenly distributed in the ice cream.

1. In a small, heavy-based saucepan, slowly dissolve the sugar in 150ml water. Boil for exactly 3 minutes, then remove from the heat and cool for 1 minute.

2. Put the egg yolks into a large bowl with the ground ginger, whisk lightly and pour into the hot sugar syrup (do not allow the whisk to touch the syrup, or the cold metal will cool the syrup and it will stick to the whisk). Add the stem ginger.

3. Lightly whip the cream until thickened but still just liquid. When the egg-yolk mix is cool, fold in the cream, then pour into a plastic container and freeze.

4. When the ice cream is frozen but is not yet rock-hard, take it out, chop it into chunks and whizz in a food processor. This will beat more air into it and ensure the ginger doesn't sink to the bottom. (In the absence of a food processor, stir the ice cream with a fork when it is half-frozen.) Return to the freezer.

5. Remove the ice cream from the freezer half an hour before it is to be eaten.

If scooping the ice cream into a bowl for serving, put the empty bowl in the freezer in advance to chill.

Vanilla ice-box biscuits

Makes 30

115g butter

225g caster sugar

1 medium egg

1 tsp vanilla extract

½ tsp finely grated lemon zest

275g strong white flour

¼ tsp salt

2 tsp baking powder

caster sugar or 100g blanched flaked almonds to decorate

(Pictured overleaf.)

Baked biscuits, if kept in an airtight container, do keep very well, but freshly baked ones are something else. You can keep the roll of dough in the freezer, then thaw, slice and bake as needed, refreezing whatever you didn't slice straight away. (Yes, I know we are told not to refreeze things, but that's mainly because manufacturers don't trust us to be sensible and are covering their backs. This is perfectly safe, I promise!)

1. Beat the butter and sugar until light and fluffy.

2. Beat in the egg. Add the vanilla and lemon zest.

3. Sift the flour, salt and baking powder together and stir into the butter mixture to make a soft dough.

4. Shape the dough into long rolls about 4cm (1½ in) in diameter. (If the dough is too soft to roll, resist the temptation to add extra flour. Instead, chill it until it is firm enough to handle.) Wrap the rolls in greaseproof or waxed paper, or in cling film, and refrigerate overnight.

5. When ready to bake, heat the oven to 200°C/fan 180°C/gas mark 6. Unwrap a roll and slice as many thinnest-possible discs from it as you need. Put them, spaced slightly apart, on a lightly greased baking tray. Return the rest of the dough roll(s) to the fridge or freezer.

6. Either sprinkle the biscuits with caster sugar for a sandy texture, or press flaked almonds into them.

7. Bake for about 8 minutes. Remove from the oven and allow to cool for a minute or two before transferring to a wire rack.

> If using the dough within days, keep the rolls in the fridge. Any longer than 3 days, they should go into the freezer and will need thawing (preferably in the fridge) before slicing.

Tropical spiced fruit salad

Serves 8

For the syrup

1 lime

100g caster sugar

3 black peppercorns

2 cloves

3 star anise

a small handful of mint leaves

For the fruit salad

1 pineapple

2 passion fruit

2 kiwi fruit

1 mango

1 papaya

100g physalis

2–3 tbsp mint leaves, roughly chopped

I sometimes serve this on Christmas night, when everyone is overfull of turkey and plum pud. Fruit salads can be boring in winter without our wonderful summer fruits, but a mix of tropical fruit with a hint of festive spice is great.

1. For the syrup, thinly pare the rind from the lime and put it in a small saucepan. Squeeze the lime juice into the pan and add the other syrup ingredients and 150ml water. Bring to the boil, then simmer for 6–8 minutes until the volume is reduced by roughly half and the consistency is syrupy. Remove from the heat and allow to cool to room temperature.

2. Prepare all the fruit, adding it to a large serving bowl as you go. Cut the leaves and base off the pineapple. Stand the pineapple up on a board and, using a sharp knife, cut downwards to slice the peel from the fruit. Still holding the fruit upright, slice downwards on all four sides to remove the flesh, leaving the woody core. Cut the flesh into 1–2cm (½ in) cubes. To prepare the passion fruit, cut them in half with a sharp knife and scoop out the edible seeds and juicy flesh that surrounds them.

3. Cut each end off the kiwi fruit, then peel off the fuzzy skin with a vegetable peeler or knife. Cut the flesh into slices.

4. Peel the mango with a sharp knife. Slice through the mango as close as you can to the stone, to remove the 'cheeks' on each side. Cut these into 1cm (½ in) cubes, then slice and cube remaining flesh left on the stone.

5. Slice the papaya in half lengthways, scrape out the seeds and scoop out the flesh with a melon baller. With the physalis, simply pull back the papery calyx to reveal the fruit and cut in half.

6. Pour the syrup, with its flavourings, over the fruit and gently combine. Sprinkle with the chopped mint.

> Bananas, melons and pomegranates are good too. Add the bananas as late as possible, lest they go brown, and scatter pomegranate seeds over the top.
>
> A good splash of rum in the fruit salad is good too. Glorious, even.

Baked peaches in rum

Serves 4

3 tbsp runny honey

2 tbsp butter

1 vanilla pod, split, or 2 tsp vanilla paste

a good pinch of salt

2 tbsp rum

4 peaches, halved and stoned

40g pecans, roughly chopped

crème fraiche to serve

This is the simplest of dishes. If we have a lot of friends and family to feed, I know this will be a winner. I do one version with rum, and one without for the children, though it has to be said that children will happily wolf down the grown-ups' version. In fact, the alcohol will be driven off in the cooking, just leaving behind the flavour, so you needn't worry. It's just that I'm too mean to splash out on rum for children!

1. Heat the oven to 180°C/fan 160°C/gas mark 4.

2. Warm the honey, butter, vanilla, salt and rum in a small saucepan until just bubbling.

3. Set the peaches, cut side up, in a baking dish and pour over the syrup. Bake for 20 minutes, or until the peaches are softened, a little caramelized and sticky.

4. Toss the pecans in a dry frying pan over a medium heat until just toasted. Remove and discard the vanilla pod.

5. Remove the peaches from the oven and sprinkle with the pecans. Serve two peach halves per person with a good spoonful of the syrup and a dollop of crème fraiche.

There are endless variations on this theme of boozy baked fruit. Nectarines with amaretto; halved plums with damson liqueur, half-apples with Calvados. Almost anything you can think of would probably be good, especially if served with ice cream.

Normandy tart

Serves 10–12

For the pastry

225g plain flour plus extra for dusting

140g cold butter plus extra for greasing

1 medium egg

a pinch of salt

60g caster sugar

For the almond filling (frangipane)

170g butter

170g caster sugar

170g ground almonds

2 large eggs

1 tbsp Calvados, kirsch, or whatever liqueur you like

a few drops of almond essence

For the glaze

3–4 small red dessert apples, skin left on, cored and halved

100g smooth apricot jam

juice of ½ lemon

I've been demonstrating this dish for years, and it always gets a gratifying round of applause when it comes out of the oven. It's a piece of cake (or tart) to make if you have a food processor.

1. Heat the oven to 200°C/fan 180°C/gas mark 6, and put a baking sheet on the middle shelf to heat. Lightly butter a 26cm (10in) loose-bottomed tart tin and dust with flour, tipping out any excess.

2. For the pastry, whizz all the ingredients together in a food processor until the dough forms a ball. Roll it out into a thin, even round big enough to line the tin. Lift the pastry by rolling it round the rolling pin and then unrolling it over the tin. Don't worry if the pastry cracks. It is so rich that you can just use your fingers to patch any gaps. Ease the pastry into the corners, then roll your rolling pin firmly across the top, to trim away any excess pastry.

3. For the almond filling, whizz everything in the processor (no need to wash the bowl after the pastry). Spread it evenly over the pastry case.

4. Lay an apple half, cut-side down, on a board and slice across finely, keeping the slices in order and in their original half-apple shape. With the heel of your hand, gently push the half-apple so the slices separate a little and lie flat, neatly overlapping each other. Using a palette knife or spatula to help, lift the sliced half-apples and place them on the frangipane in concentric circles, starting at the rim. Gently press them into the frangipane.

5. Set the tart in the middle of the oven, on the hot baking sheet, and bake for 30 minutes. Turn the oven down to 180°C/fan 160°C/gas mark 4 and bake for another 15–20 minutes or until the filling is set and brown. Then remove from the oven.

6. For the glaze, melt the jam with the lemon juice in a small heavy-based saucepan. Brush or spoon carefully all over the apples and filling.

7. When the tart is still just warm, check that the edges of the pastry are not stuck anywhere to the metal ring (over-enthusiastic jamming can cause a problem), then ease the tart from the tin. Serve warm with cream or ice cream for a pudding, or cold in a thin slice for tea.

Chocolate and macadamia biscotti

Makes 30

200g plain flour

50g cocoa powder

1½ tsp baking powder

a pinch of salt

150g caster sugar

100g macadamias, roughly chopped

2 large eggs, beaten

Biscotti in a packet from Italy are delicious – but not cheap, so I think it's worth making your own. They keep well in an airtight tin and are delicious with ice creams and other creamy puds in need of a contrasting crunch.

1. Heat the oven to 190°C/fan 170°C/gas mark 5. Line a baking sheet with baking parchment.

2. Combine everything except the eggs in a big bowl. Gradually add the beaten eggs to the mixture and combine to make a fairly stiff dough.

3. Divide the dough into three and form into sausage-shaped logs about 20cm x 4cm (8in x 1½in). Put on the baking sheet, spacing them roughly 6cm (2½in) apart, and bake for 20 minutes.

4. Wait until just cool enough to handle, then gently cut the logs on the diagonal to form 1cm (½in) slices (a serrated bread knife works best). Return the biscotti to the baking sheet (you may now need a second one) and bake for a further 10 minutes, turning them over after 5 minutes.

The classic twice-baked biscotti are often dunked in the sweet after-dinner wine called Vin Santo. This chocolate version is good dunked in coffee or coffee liqueur. Or, if you are too posh to dunk, eaten alongside.

Pink peppercorn and chocolate mousse cake

Serves 8

75g pecans

1 tsp pink peppercorns, plus extra to serve

150g salted butter plus extra for greasing

250g good-quality dark chocolate

150g caster sugar

5 large eggs, separated

1 tbsp whisky

a pinch of salt

icing sugar to serve

This recipe was devised by my friend and collaborator Georgina Fuggle (she has cooked every single recipe in this book, some of them three times), and it is astonishingly good. I have yet to see someone refuse a second slice. The texture is like a cross between a brownie and a chocolate mousse, and the little kick from the pink peppercorns is surprising and delightful.

1. Lightly butter and line a 23cm (9 in) round spring-form cake tin with baking parchment. Heat the oven to 160°C/fan 140°C/gas mark 3.

2. Tip the pecans onto a baking tray and transfer to the oven to toast for 6–7 minutes. Blitz to a fine dust in a food processor, then set aside. Crush the peppercorns in a pestle and mortar until fine (failing that, bash them with the end of a rolling pin in a small bowl).

3. Melt the butter and chocolate in a heatproof bowl set over simmering water, or in the microwave. Remove from the heat and mix in 60g of the sugar. Then stir in the egg yolks, pecans, most of the peppercorns and the whisky.

4. In another large bowl, add the salt to the egg whites and use an electric whisk to beat them to soft peaks. Whisk in half the remaining sugar, until the mixture will stand up in peaks when the whisk is lifted, then add the rest of the sugar. Whisk again until stiff and glossy. Stir a spoon of this meringue into the chocolate mixture to loosen it a bit, then carefully fold in the rest (be gentle, you want to avoid bashing out all the air you've carefully incorporated). Pour the batter into the tin, level the top and bake for 25 minutes.

5. Leave the cake to cool in the tin, on a wire rack, for 10 minutes. It will sink dramatically – but don't worry. Once cool, remove the cake from the tin and dust with icing sugar and a scrunch of pink peppercorns.

> This cake has never lasted a day in my house, but I'm told it freezes well. As it's quick and easy to make, why not double up the quantities, and freeze one to have later, perhaps to do duty as a pudding with cream?

Thank you

I should first thank the *Great British Menu* chefs and the *The Great British Bake Off* team, especially my fellow judge Paul Hollywood and the *Bake-Off* contestants. Their inspired creativity and love of cooking was the catalyst that got me back to food writing.

I should also thank a bunch of good friends and great people who made *Prue* happen. First and foremost, Georgina Fuggle, herself a published food writer, who has endlessly tested, retested and perfected all the recipes in the book. And then David Hawson for his captivating watercolours; David Loftus, for his mouth-watering photographs, which he'd not have achieved without the help of food stylist Pip Spence and her assistant Libby Silbermann who, while following my recipes to the letter, nonetheless made them look more delicious than I could; James Verity of Superfantastic Design for the overall look of what I hope you agree is a beautiful book; Jane Turnbull, great agent and lovely friend; Carole Tonkinson, ever-supportive boss of Bluebird at Pan Macmillan who commissioned the book and has overseen its progress like a nanny; Martha Burley, Bluebird's brilliant cookery editor; my long-suffering and overworked PA, Francisca Sankson, who has read every word, corrected my punctuation and caught many a boo-boo; Lyn Pearse, her assistant and my some-time housekeeper, who keeps the home fires burning. She's only matched in this department by my husband John Playfair, who has other virtues too, like making us all laugh and happily eating the failures with only slightly less pleasure than the successes. Thanks to all. for making the production of my first cookbook in 25 years an absolute pleasure. It's been such fun, I might even write another one.

Index

Note: page numbers in *italics* refer to illustrations.

About Prue

Prue Leith has been at the top of the British food scene for nearly sixty years. She has seen huge success not only as founder of the renowned Leith's School of Food and Wine, but also as a caterer, restaurateur, teacher, TV cook, food journalist, novelist, and cookery book author. She's also been a leading figure in campaigns to improve food in schools, hospitals and in the home. Well known as a judge on *The Great British Menu*, now she is a judge on the nation's favourite TV programme, *The Great British Bake Off*. Prue was born in South Africa and lives in the UK.

First published 2018 by Bluebird
an imprint of Pan Macmillan
20 New Wharf Road, London N1 9RR
Associated companies throughout the world www.panmacmillan.com

ISBN   978-1-5098-9148-1

9 8 7 6 5 4 3 2 1

A CIP catalogue record for this book is available from the British Library.

Printed and bound in Italy.

Publisher Carole Tonkinson
Senior Editor Martha Burley
Editor Hockley Raven Spare
Senior Production Controller Sarah Badhan
Art Direction & Design Superfantastic
Food Styling Pip Spence
Prop Styling Lydia Brun
Paintings David Hawson

Visit www.panmacmillan.com to read more about all our books and to buy them. You will
also find features, author interviews and news of any author events, and you can sign up for
e-newsletters so that you're always first to hear about our new releases.